Barcelona
architecture guide
1929-2002

Editorial Gustavo Gili, SA

08029 Barcelona   Rosselló, 87-89. Tel. 93 322 81 61

Antoni González / Raquel Lacuesta

Barcelona
architecture guide
1929-2002

GG®

new edition

To the memory of
Manuel Gimeno Bartolomé,
architect (1947-1993)

Cover Illustration:

German Pavilion at the 1929 International
Exibition in Barcelona.
Ludwig Mies van der Rohe, architect
Photograph by **Eloi Bonjoch**

Translation:
Graham Thomson

© Editorial Gustavo Gili, SA, Barcelona 2002

Printed in Spain
ISBN: 84-252-1894-2
Depósito legal: B.: 4.221 - 2002
Printed: Gráficas 92, SA (Rubí)

Index

Authors and collaborators

Antoni González Moreno-Navarro

Architect (Barcelona, 1970). Restorer of monuments. Director of the Arxiu Històric d'Arquitectura, Urbanisme i Disseny (AHUAD) of the Col.legi d'Arquitectes de Catalunya (1975). Since 1981, Head of the Servei del Patrimoni Arquitectònic Local, Diputació de Barcelona.
President of the Academia del Partal (Independent Association of Professional Restorers of Monuments).

Raquel Lacuesta Contreras

Degrees in History of Art (1973) and Philosophy and Science of Education (1987) from the Universitat de Barcelona. Collaborator, Arxiu Històric d'Arquitectura, Urbanisme i Disseny of the Col.legi d'Arquitectes de Catalunya (1973-1978). Since 1996, in charge of the documentation and diffusion department of the Servei del Patrimoni Arquitectònic Local of the Diputació de Barcelona.
Founder member of the Academia del Partal.

Antoni González and Raquel Lacuesta have previously worked together as authors and editors of the following books:

La Sagrada Familia, ¿para qué y para quién? (1976)
Inventario del patrimonio arquitectónico de Barcelona (1980)
1380-1980, seis siglos de protección del patrimonio arquitectónico de Cataluña (1984)
32 monumentos catalanes (1985)
La arquitectura en la historia de Cataluña (1987)
Com i per a qui restaurem (1990)
Arquitectura modernista en Cataluña (1997)
El palau Güell (2001)

Drawings

Sònia Blasco, Rubén O. Montero, Txetxu Sanz.

Collaborators

(Documentation): Francesc Balañà Comas, architect; Maria Antònia Carrasco Martí (MA in Art History); Maria Dolors Forés Mendialdúa (MA in Modern History).

Photographs

Montserrat Baldomà: 13b, 16, 17, 18a, 19a, 20b, 21b, 29b, 33a, 36b, 48a, 51, 56b, 60, 64, 72, 78b, 79b, 85a, 85b, 87, 90b, 92, 105b, 106c, 115, 116, 127, 128b, 129, 132, 133, 134, 141, 143, 144c, 146, 148, 165b, 171a, 174, 175, 176, 177, 178, 179, 180, 181a, 182, 183, 188.
Jaume Orpinell: 12a, 15, 18a, 19b, 20a, 22, 24, 28, 29a, 30, 31a, 38a, 38b, 43, 44, 48b, 50a, 52, 57a, 58b, 59b, 68a, 69, 71, 78a, 81, 93a, 98, 102, 105c, 106a, 106b, 107, 109, 110, 112a, 114a, 114b, 114c, 117a, 118, 120, 121, 122, 123, 126, 128a, 130, 135, 136, 137, 138, 139, 140, 142, 144b, 145, 147, 150, 151a, 152, 153, 154, 155, 157, 158, 159, 161a, 162, 163, 164, 165a, 166a, 167b, 168, 169a, 169b, 170a, 170b, 172, 173, 184, 186, 189, 190 (Xavier Basiana), 197.

AHUAD: 34, 37b; José María Alguersuari: 194; J. Artigues: 185c; Ajuntament de Barcelona: 125; Alejo Bagué: 191; Albert Bastardes: 35a, 37a; Arxiu GMN: 10a, 10b, 11, 12b, 12c, 14, 18b, 19c, 20b, 21a, 25, 26, 27, 32, 33b, 35b, 36a, 38c, 40, 41, 46a, 47a, 48c, 49, 53b, 56a, 58a, 59a, 63, 64, 65, 67, 70, 74a, 74b, 75, 76, 79b, 80, 83, 84, 85c, 86, 88, 94, 95a, 96a, 96b, 97a, 101b, 104a, 104b, 105a, 124a, 124b, 144a, 151b, 153, 160b, 161b, 166b, 167a; Francesc Balañà: 156; F. Català Roca: 23, 46b, 50b, 53a, 57b, 61, 62, 73, 77a, 77b, 89b, 93b, 95b, 97b, 99, 102b; CB fotos: 101a; Julio Cunill: 196a, 196b; J. Cebollero: 39, 54; Foto 18x24: 108; Foto Sender: 67b; Ferran Freixa, 171b; Pau Giralt (Fundació Caixa de Catalunya), 181b; Cinto Hom: 187; Jovan Horvat: 193; Duccio Malagamba: 195; Maspons & Ubiña: 47b, 82; Jordi Nieva: 112b; Serrat & Marqués: 89a, 100b; Jaume Soler: 119; Tavisa: 192; Elías Torres: 185a, 185b; Serena Vergano: 79a; Adolfo Zerkowitz: 13a.

Introduction

1929 and 1992 were two moments of great significance in the urban evolution of Barcelona. The first saw the opening of the International Exhibition, a great exposition originally conceived in 1917 in less ambitious terms (as an Electrical Industries Exhibition) which the military regime newly installed in Spain in 1923 decided to promote onto a more profitable scale. This provided the opportunity for the city –which has always made the most of such occasions to set itself in order and make some long-cherished dream come true– to develop the emblematic promontory lapped by the sea that we Barcelonese proudly refer to as the *Muntanya de Montjuïc* and to complete the laying out of avenues and promenades envisaged in the 1859 Cerdà Plan or one of several subsequent urban plans.

In 1992 it was the celebration of the summer Olympic Games that was to provide the impetus to complete a process of urban renewal that, thanks to Spain's newly restored democracy, had been initiated before the city's Olympic nomination. This time the urban reforms were more ambitious. In addition to the different parts of the city directly affected by the celebration of the Games, there were major works of infrastructure (drainage, communications, services) affecting the whole city and, once again, implementation of various projects first posited in the Cerdà Plan that had been awaiting a suitable moment for almost a hundred and fifty years.

On these two occasions, architecture inevitably assumed an essential role. The new exhibition pavilions, hotels, sports facilities, temporary residences an so on transformed the urban landscape. On both occasions, the change was not merely temporary, since Barcelona has (or at any rate had, until quite recently) a tendency to make the transitory permanent, not so much for reasons of economy as of signification and symbolism. A considerable number of our present-day public facilities are to be found housed in buildings constructed for the 1929 exhibition that we have managed to conserve. Something similar occurred with the buildings produced for the 1992 Olympic Games.

The two clusters of Barcelona architectures that came into being around these great civic occasions include amongst them works of major cultural importance, not only locally but internationally. A prime example would be the German Pavilion for the 1929 Exhibition, designed by Mies van der Rohe, one of the essential achievements of the Modern Movement. (Let us leave history to judge in the fullness of time whether any of the '92 Olympic constructions is worthy of a similar assessment.)

These two dates thus appeared to us to be sufficiently significant as to mark the beginning and end of a period in Barcelona's architecture; a period that we in turn divided into three parts in an attempt at reflecting the evolution which that architecture –itself the reflection of broader patterns of social change– has experienced for more than seventy years.

The first part (1929-1950) deals with the group of works belonging to what is known as *Noucentista* architecture, a chronological period whose beginning in fact dates from several years earlier, and coincides with the decline of the *Modernisme* that occupies such a key position in the history of Catalan and particularly of Barcelonese architecture. With regard to the closing date of this subperiod, 1950 –and not 1939, the end of the Civil War– is the year we consider as best representing the irruption of a profoundly innovative change in our architecture.

The years 1951 to 1978 (when the new democratic Constitution was established) comprise the second part, embracing a highly diverse series of architectures –ranging from those of Grup R and their contemporaries to those of the very craft-based "Barcelona School" and its offshoots in the seventies– with one common denominator: the simultaneous pursuit of both an opening-up to the outside world and a specific and unique identity within the context of an evidently difficult political situation.

The third and last part (1978-2002) opens with the advent of new phenomena produced by the new political situation: an increased sensitivity to the past, the greater number and scale of public initiatives –noting the special impact on the city of the Olympic Games– and the incorporation into this public endeavour of architects with a highly cultured approach to the discipline. The edition we are now presenting coincides with the preparation of "Barcelona 2004: A World Forum of Cultures", which also implies important urban changes.

Some observations

Evidently, the term Barcelona architecture should be understood as covering everything constructed in the metropolitan area of Barcelona. We therefore wish to make explicitly clear at this point that in strictly limiting the scope of the present guide, for reasons of space, to the area within the city boundaries, we have been obliged to leave out (or at least not give full attention to) a number of buildings of fundamental importance in the Barcelona architecture of this period.

As for the transport services we indicate as offering the most convenient means of reaching the locations, in addition to the Metro and FF.CC. local rail systems we have considered only daytime bus routes, and then only those with a stop very close to the buildings in question.

The bibliography which is appended at the end of the book is a selection which for reasons of space does not include monographic studies of the buildings; however, most of these studies are to be found in the specialist journals and magazines cited, noting those issues which feature material of this kind.

Antoni González, Raquel Lacuesta.
Barcelona, 2002.

1929-1950

In the first decade of the 20th century, with the spread of *Modernisme* throughout the country, the social and cultural conditions were being generated that would bring about the decline of that movement and usher in one of the most complex periods in the history of Catalan architecture.

1906 marks the advent of the wider dissemination of the new social and cultural ideas which, promulgated by the thinker Eugeni d'Ors, were to provide the ideological framework for the modernizing endeavours of the industrial bourgeoisie, the first institutional manifestation of which was an early move towards greater political autonomy (the Mancomunitat de Catalunya, 1917-1923), soon repressed by the first of the new century's dictatorships (under General Primo de Rivera, 1923-1930). A few years later, in the more propitious climate of a changed State regime (the Second Republic, 1931-1939), Catalonia attempted a more profound form of autonomy with greater popular support (the Generalitat de Catalunya, 1932-1939), interrupted in its turn by a new dictatorship (that of General Franco, 1937-1975) following a Civil War (1936-1939) that had been marked by a struggle for a more radical social revolution.

Catalan architecture, responsive to these internal social and cultural upheavals and to the innovative movements in architecture then coming to the fore in Europe and North America –throughout a period that extends approximately from 1919 (although the present guide, for the reasons outlined above, takes 1929 as its starting point) until 1950 (since we consider that the Civil War, as we hope to demonstrate, was not responsible for any appreciable reversal in our architecture, at least in its creative aspects)– embraced a whole spectrum of programmes and languages. None of these can lay exclusive claim, either in quality or representative capacity, to the period or to the various possible subperiods which together constitute Noucentista architecture, a concept which should thus be seen as applying to an ampler spectrum than its purely Catalan manifestations or those of, for example, the Italian Novecento.

Noucentista architectures

When Eugeni d'Ors began to air his views, it soon became apparent that *Modernista* architecture (then dominant throughout Catalonia) was out of step with the new spirit. Nicolás M. Rubió Tudurí –self-proclaimed "unofficial Noucentista "– analysed the situation in these terms:

"In spite of how things might seem today, regarded from a distance of half a century, the triumph of *Modernisme* was neither easily nor fully accomplished here, if it can indeed be called a triumph. Gaudianism and *Modernisme* were always regarded by the main body of Barcelona society as heretical. Some were even heard to say that both 'degraded' the city... The Palau de la Música Catalana, in particular, was the target of diatribes and vituperations on every evening there was a concert... the city repudiated the new style and, by extension, every other innovation in architecture. An anxiously visceral urge to get back to classical architecture –"what has always been"– gripped Barcelona, an anxiety that materialized in a 'revolutionary return to the purest and clearest wellsprings of the Renaissance'".

In point of fact, the architectonic language that proved the most able interpreter of the spirit inspired by Eugeni d'Ors (and the one most frequently associated with *Noucentisme*) was that of 14th -and 15th- century Florentine classicism. The new Benedictine monastery of Montserrat (now the María Reina parish church) on the carretera d'Esplugues, built by Rubió Tudurí himself in 1922, is the perfect example of the search for order, measure, clarity and serenity which brought together, on ethico-architectonic or ethico-ideological common ground, the younger generation of architects and the cultural tribunes of the Catalan industrial bourgeoisie.

The Brunelleschian model was not, however, exclusive to those early years of *Noucentisme*. It extends throughout the whole of the period we are considering here, and for a dozen years after the end of the war buildings in this style were still being constructed in Barcelona; for example, the church of Sant Miquel dels Sants in c/ Escorial, by the architect Fisas. In relation to this classicism, we also need to consider the academicism of Duran Reynals –arguably, together with Rubió Tudurí and Josep Maria Pericas, one of the ablest and most highly qualified architects of post-Modernista Barcelona– and of some of his followers: an academicism that also continued into the second half of the century.

Casa Pericas. Av. Diagonal, 389. 1917. Josep M. Pericas.

Pere Vila school. 1921. Josep Goday Casals.

Between tradition and the avant-gardes

Another of the roads towards the "normalization" of architectonic creation after the "Modernista excess" was to turn to local tradition; not, this time, the styles of the Mediaeval period but the simple, reassuring forms of popular architecture or the highly suggestive forms of the vernacular baroque.

The Casa Company (c/ Buenos Aires, 56-58), constructed by Puig Cadafalch in 1911, is a first announcement of this looking to the past, although in this case there is also some influence from contemporary Central European architecture, while the schools designed by Goday around 1920 draw their references from more recent historical images, such as the churches and palaces of an 18th- century Catalan baroque which also transformed many existing farmhouses, thus readily lending itself to the signalling of associations with the rural world.

Alongside these evocations of indigenous, we should note the eclectic nature of the use made of a classicist repertoire present in Catalan architecture over more than a century with no effective resolution in terms of continuity, despite changes in intentions and the emphasis given to the utilization of its elements, the adaptation of –by combination with– other current elements and the highlighting, to greater or lesser effect, of imported stylistic devices at different moments. The Casa Puig (c/ Provença, 231) of 1917, by Puig Cadafalch, the Casa Cambó (Via

Casa Cambó. 1921-1925. Adolf Florensa.

Cine Coliseum. 1923. Francesc de P. Nebot.

María Reina parish church, 1922. Nicolás M. Rubió Tudurí.

The 1929 Exhibition. Plaza del Universo.

Hotel for the 1929 Exhibition (demolished in 1991). Nicolás M. Rubió Tudurí.

Echoes of the Exhibition. Art Déco illuminations in the plaza de Catalunya on May 20th, 1930.

Laietana, 30) of 1921-1925 by A. Florensa, and the Fomento de Obras y Construcciones building (c/ Balmes, 36-42) by J. Torres Grau (1924-1925) are examples from immediately prior to the period of the present study that were to enjoy continuity thereafter by way of a great number of lesser works.

During the twenties, this eclecticism with classical roots took a rhetorical and grandiloquent turn in many works which freely mixed different stylistic elements: baroque, Greco-Roman, plateresque, and the "French national style" of Charles Garnier. Good examples of this are the Cine Coliseum (Gran Via Corts Catalanes, 595) by Francesc de P. Nebot (1923), the Casa Almirall (Diagonal, 433-439) by Francesc Guàrdia Vial (1928-1932) or the contemporaneous Unión y Fénix Español building.

With all the caution necessary in advancing this kind of hypothesis, we might incline to the view that, just as there was an evident relationship between Florentine classicism and the mentality of the cultured Catalanist bourgeoisie, so too this monumentalist eclecticism was very much in tune with the social and aesthetic attitudes of the dictatorship of General Primo de Rivera. Perhaps for this reason, the fact that the Barcelona Exhibition of 1929 (an undertaking first formulated fifteen years earlier) was held at a time when the first moves towards autonomy for Catalonia had been frustrated, had a decisive influence on the architectonic rhetoric of the Exhibition and on the fact

Echoes of the Exhibition. Vestibule. Paseo Sant Joan, 204. 1930. J. Gumà Cuevas.

that, thanks to the extensive popular echoing of this rhetoric, it was soon to be found to every part of the city, almost always in the mediocre form of a "consumer monumentalism" that endured until the early 1950s. Alongside these very diverse architectures, from around the middle of the second decade of the century Catalonia began to see the emergence of works couched in a surprising new language, assimilable neither to Modernisme –despite its debt to the conceptual contributions of the great Catalan architects of previous decades– nor to classicism. Nor were they the product of some new artistic and aesthetic climate. Perhaps their common distinctive feature was no more than a formal connection with the European avant-garde movements, an influence which the younger Catalan architects absorbed on trips abroad or from the magazines.

We can not talk of definite schools or tendencies as such (these architects designed simultaneous works in different languages, exposing the lack of "stylistic militancy" so characteristic of the *Noucentistes*), but the results were in many cases brilliant. In the city of Barcelona we must mention, prior to 1929, the El Carme parish church (c/ Bisbe Laguarda, 1) by Josep Maria Pericas (constructed between 1910 and 1949), and two other works by the same architect: the Casa Pericas (Av. Diagonal, 389; Còrsega, 319) dating from 1917, and the Casa Mitjans (c/ Menor de Sarrià, 6) from 1925.

Of the buildings already in existence at the start of the period we shall go on to consider here (on which Art Déco exercised a decisive influence), it would be unforgivable to overlook a magnigificent work of architecture which the city, even after the restoration of democracy: the Seix y Barral publishing house (c/ Provença, 217), designed by Mestres Fossas, built in 1930 and demolished in 1978.

The imprint of Rationalism

The third decade of the century brought the consolidation of a profound renovation of European architecture, the symptoms of which were already apparent in the previous decade. Young architects (Le Corbusier, who published his *Vers une architecture* in 1925 and constructed the Ville Savoye in 1928; Walter Gropius; Mies van der Rohe, who gave Barcelona a masterpiece with his German Pavilion for the 1929 Exhibition), some of them very young (Alvar Aalto built his masterly Paimio sanatorium in 1930), called for a thorough review of the theoretical concepts underlying the practice of architecture and, by extension, its language.

This innovative impulse was given specific articulation in three essential principles: as a general objective, the population must find in the built environment better conditions for individual

Radio Barcelona. 1926-1929. Nicolás M. Rubió Tudurí.

and collective development, this implying the need to rethink the premises governing the design of housing, of social amenities and of cities. As an indispensable means to achieving this end, the construction industry was to be revolutionized, to allow the introduction of the technical systems required to build this new architecture. And as a consequence of this, a new architectural language would emerge, capable of expressing these innovative intentions, propositions, contents and technical methods.

The Catalan architectural avantgarde immediately recognized and declared its affinities with this movement (and, once again, through Rubió Tudurí, designer of the Radio Barcelona building constructed on the summit of Tibidabo between 1926 and 1929) and went on to found an organized group, the GATCPAC. However, the three objectives were not all realised to the same degree. The renovation of programmatic contents was largely conditioned by political factors. Only in a progressive context, during the years of the Generalitat and the Republic, was it possible to undertake such a radical transformation of housing and public facilities and the collective enjoyment of natural and built resources. Previously, the renovation of contents had only been able to contemplate the improvement of the homes of the middle classes, which was what in fact occurred.

The revolution in construction, especially in the field of technologies, could not be more than a declaration of objectives (attempts at transforming the sector's existing structures were extensively mediated by the facts of civil war and revolutionary social change). As regards the new language that was to be the formal expression of all of this, the few built examples (the period of time in which this architecture can be said to have flourished in Catalonia is extremely short — a decade at most) constituted more a manifesto of aims and objectives than the expression of tangible results.

Rationalism, the name by which this cultural phenomenon is generally known, played a decisive part in shaping the future of Catalan architectural culture, but it was also decisive for architecture as a whole. Of rationalism, what the system adopted as its own were the profitable advantages it made available to the property market, irrespective of whether or not it offered any social benefit. It could be said that the sad architecture which quantitatively dominated the years of economic boom following the Second World War was the bastard offspring of that spirit of innovation.

Postwar architecture
We have already mentioned our reluctance to look on the years of the Spanish Civil War as determining any significant change in the formal aspects of

Editorial Seix y Barral. 1930 (demolished 1978). J. Mestres Fossas.

14

architecture in Catalonia. On the one hand, we must not forget that the underlying mentalities which effectively defined most of the architectonic languages in use before the war were still (like the local bourgeoisie, which never lost its hegemonic role in society) in place after the conflict had ended. In fact, these languages evolved smoothly and continuously, and showed no signs of exhaustion –such as the rhetoric that usually announces the end– until the early fifties, when certain younger architects succeeded in interesting the cultured minority within the middle class in the project of formal innovation.

The continuity of classicism is apparent (there is no contradiction, for example, between Duran Reynals' pre- and postwar work), and the different strains of eclecticism also survived –duly adapted to a logical evolution– in residential (El Rancho Grande, at Via Augusta, 170-180 and c/ Muntaner, 367, by Joaquim Lloret Homs, 1944, or the Frare Negre at c/ Balmes, 429-445, by Eusebi Bona, 1940) and institutional architecture (such as the Banco Vitalicio or the Instituto Nacional de Previsión, both by Bonet Garí). As regards the question of the possible continuity that orthodox rationalism might have enjoyed, since the decisive impact of the disappearance of its leading practitioners is beyond dispute, we shall never be able to assert that this continuity would have been assured had the Civil War had a different outcome; that, at least, seems to emerge from consideration of the process in other European countries.

On the other hand, it is highly problematic to attempt to speak –in terms of Catalonia, at least– of stylistic repression by the new regime, or even of a new "Francoist architecture" imposed by power. Some light may be shed on the former issue by the book *Homenaje de Cataluña liberada a su caudillo Franco* (Homage of a liberated Catalonia to her leader Franco), published in 1939, which eulogizes Modernism and Functionalism as supreme moments of the "principle of creation and invention" in architecture. The validity of the second assertion would seem to be borne out by the diversity of languages utilized in the small number of public buildings constructed by the new regime, including some works of genuine interest, such as the Officers' Residence (Av. Diagonal, 666) designed by Manuel de Solà-Morales Rosselló in 1939-1940.

Over the next thirty pages, we have opted to present the most significant works of this complex period, grouped not on the basis of the formal tendencies or conceptual programmes referred to above, but set out in chronological sequence, in the conviction that the evident sense of confusion this chronological order is likely to arouse will at least be analogous to the sensations of those who lived through the simultaneity of diverse languages that characterized the *Noucentista* period.

Officers' residence. Av. Diagonal. 1939-1940. Manuel de Solá-Morales Rosselló.

1
Barcelona International Exhibition 1923-1929

Parque de Montjuïc - Plaza de España
Bus 13, 27, 30, 55, 61. Metro L1, L3 (España)

The original scheme to make the mountain of Montjuïc the site for a proposed Electrical Industries exposition in 1917 –to a General Plan drawn up by the architect Josep Puig Cadafalch– suffered a series of setbacks of various kinds, and in due course the venture metamorphosed into the International Exhibition which occupied the space during 1929 and 1930. Construction of the new road network had begun in 1915, under the direction of Josep Amargós, and almost at the same time the engineer Jean C. N. Forestier was commissioned to carry out the landscaping of the site, with the collaboration of the architect Nicolás M. Rubió Tudurí.

Of note amongst the buildings constructed on the occasion of the great exhibition and still standing today –a very good sample of what we have described as monumental eclecticism– are the palaces of Alfons XII and Victòria Eugènia (Plaza del Marquès de Foronda, Puig Cadafalch, 1923-1928); the Palacio Nacional, now the Museo de Arte de Catalunya (Plaza del Mirador, Enric Català, Pedro Cendoya and Pere Domènech Roura, 1925-1929); the Palace of the City of Barcelona (Josep Goday Casals, 1928); the Casa de la Premsa press headquarters, now used by the Guàrdia Urbana metropolitan police (c/ de la Guàrdia Urbana –formerly c/ de la Tècnica–, 1, Pere Domènech, 1926-1929); the Palace of Agriculture, today the Mercat de les Flors theatre (c/ de Lleida, Manuel M. Mayol Ferrer and Josep M. Ribas Casas, 1927-1929); the Palace of the Graphic Arts, now the city's Archaeological Museum (paseo de Santa Madrona, 39, Pelayo Martínez Paricio and Raimon Duran Reynals, 1927-1929); the Municipal Stadium (av. del Estadi, Pere Domènech, 1928); the Pueblo Español Spanish village (av. del Marquès de Comillas, Francesc Folguera and Ramon Reventós, architects, Xavier Nogués, painter, and Miquel Utrillo, 1926-1929) and the Greek Theatre (paseo de la Exposición, Forestier and Rubió Tudurí, 1929).

Towers on the Plaza de España. Ramon Reventós, architect.

Palacio Nacional. E. Català, P. Cendoya, P. Domènech, architects.

The access to the exhibition precincts from the plaza de España is signalled by two porticoed palaces, celebrating Work (Andrés Calzada and Josep M. Jujol, 1927) and Communications and Transports (by Félix de Azúa Gruart and Adolf Florensa Ferrer, 1927), and two twin towers (the work of Ramon Reventós, 1927) which frame the Reina María Cristina avenue that culminates at the Magic Fountain, designed by the engineer Carles Buïgas.

Outside of the exhibition precincts, the most significant of the buildings composing the plaza de España are the hotels; these, of unrendered brickwork with some masonry elements, were designed to harmonize with the only construction then standing on the plaza: the Arenas bullring. Of these buildings, the only ones still surviving are those marked n°. 3, converted to become the Francesc Macià public school, and n°. 4, now a police station. In the centre, between c/ Tarragona and c/ Creu Coberta, the beautiful building designed –like the other two– by Rubió Tudurí was demolished in 1991 to make way for the construction of another hotel whose volume and composition break the original unity of the plaza.

The fountain in the middle of the plaza was designed in 1928 by the architect Josep M. Jujol Gibert and restored in 1992.

Palace of the Graphic Arts (now the Archaeological Museum), P. Martínez, R. Duran Reynals, architects.

Palacio de Alfons XII, J. Puig Cadafalch, architect.

The Avila Gate of the Pueblo Español.

2

German Pavilion at the
International Exhibition   **1928-1929**

Av. Marquès de Comillas (unnumbered), Montjuïc
Ludwig Mies van der Rohe, architect
Bus 13, 61. Metro L1, L3 (Espanya)

Amid the Spanish architecture produced for the International Exhibition, opting as it did for a return to the traditional forms of the classical and the baroque, and a very varied gamut of foreign contributions, the radical project for the small German pavilion stands alone in marking a point of reference for modern European architecture.

The pavilion, occupying a site chosen in advance by Mies van der Rohe himself, and conceived as an apparently elementary interplay of planes, based its expressive power on the diaphanous character of the spaces, the quality and diversity of the materials (travertine marble, onyx, chrome and glass) and the relationship between this formal expressiveness and the crystalline setting marked by the presence of the two ponds.

The furniture –the Barcelona chair in leather and aluminium– was also designed by Mies, while the sculpture of the female figure in the inner pond was by Georg Kolbe.

The pavilion was in due course dismantled as planned at the end of the Exhibition, but in 1981 Barcelona City Council, together with the body responsible for fairs in the city, commissioned the architects Cristian Cirici Alomar, Fernando Ramos Galino and Ignasi de Solà-Morales Rubió to reconstruct it on its original site. The recreated building was inaugurated on the 2nd of June 1986, and is currently the home of the Mies van der Rohe Foundation.

The pavilion in 1929.

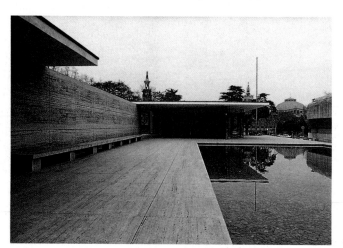

3
Estación de Francia railway station 1924-1929

Av. Marquès de l'Argentera, 6
Andreu Montaner Serra and Eduard Perxes, engineers
Pedro de Muguruza Otaño, Salvador Soteras Taberner, Raimon
Duran Reynals and Pelayo Martínez Paricio, architects
Bus 14, 39, 40, 51. Metro L4 (Barceloneta)

The old railway station, extended at various times since 1848, was the subject of major remodelling between 1926 and 1929, on the occasion of the International Exhibition. This amounted, in fact, to the replacement of the old building with a new construction conceived in terms of the model of the great railway stations of the 19th century, the last important example of which is this one in Barcelona. It was designed by Pedro de Muguruza and constructed under the direction of Salvador Soteras, an architect on the staff of the railway company.

The structure of the two great vaults over the platforms was designed by Andreu Montaner and constructed by the Catalan firm Maquinista Terrestre y Marítima, while the administrative building with its glass roof and monumental marble stairway is the work of Eduard Perxes, one of the company's engineers. The vestibule, a great space under three four-pointed vaults with their caissons supported on squinches, corresponding to the two sets of three arches which respectively constitute the station entrance and lead out to the platforms, was designed by the architects Raimon Duran and Pelayo Martínez in a classical language of deliberate monumentality.

Between 1990 and 1992, the Francia railway station, functionally superseded by the new Sants main station, was restored under the direction of the architect José Ramón Pastor González.

4
Myrurgia factory

1928-1930

C/ Mallorca, 351 - C/ Nàpols, 238
Antoni Puig Gairalt, architect
Bus 19, 33, 34, 43, 50, 54

One of the characteristic features of Antoni Puig's architecture is its incorporation of an Art Déco aesthetic, a language which in his work engages at the same time in a dialogue with the classicist spirit of early Catalan *Noucentisme* and with the new currents then moving in modern European architecture, a fact that is especially evident in the Myrurgia factory.

As this was an industrial building requiring large areas of well-lit free space, Puig approached the composition of the facades on the basis of the horizontal line which allowed him to introduce continuous bands of windows on two levels, corresponding to the production spaces of the factory floor. The access in the main facade, situated on the chamfered corner of the block, accommodates the double-flight staircase, overlooked by a sculpture by Ferran Monegal, and this taller access volume marks the axis of the building's composition. The load-bearing structure is of metal.

Antoni Puig Gairalt designed the Casa Guarro at no. 46, c/ Ample (1923-1924) and the apartment building for the Compañía de Seguros Barcelona at

no. 6, Via Laietana (1926-1928), in which elements of Catalan popular architecture are combined with Déco influences. In this latter building, the sculptural relief decorating the chamfered corner is by Joan Rebull.

Ramon Puig Gairalt, brother of Antoni, was the architect responsible for the Casa Pidelaserra at no. 178, c/ Balmes, constructed in 1932, which similarly reveals the influence of Art Déco.

5
Masana apartments

C/ Lleida, 7-11; C/ Olivera, 78; C/ Tamarit, 70
Ramon Reventós Farrarons, architect
Bus 55, 91

This apartment building is usually regarded as one of the earliest in Barcelona, if not in fact the first, in which the urban dwelling is approached with a decidedly modern mentality. For Oriol Bohigas, who considers it "the first approximation to the Bauhaus in Catalonia, with a strongly expressionist stamp", the plan designed by Reventós constitutes "the first effort towards an idea of hygiene and a reappraisal of urbanism".

In fact, this is not a single building but a complex –commissioned from Ramon Reventós between 1929 and 1931 by Josep Masana– and the same considerations should therefore be extended to the building at 68-76, c/ Olivera and 66-68, c/ Tamarit. The complex, which occupies a considerable part of the block, configures a central courtyard onto which open the courtyards of each of the properties, thus providing the rear of the building with natural light and ventilation and doing away with the need for interior light wells.

The most expressive and remarkable elements of the facade on c/ Lleida are the vertical circulation cores, above the street doors, which reveal themselves on the exterior in the form of glazed triangular galleries running the full height of the building except for the first and last floors. The facades of the other buildings are treated in similar fashion, but including the addition of balconies.

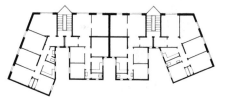

6
Casa Vilaró 1929-1930

Av. Coll del Portell, 43 and 67
Sixte Illescas Mirosa, architect
Bus 24, 31, 32, 71. Metro L3 (Lesseps)

1930 saw the foundation of the GATC-PAC (Grup d'Artistes i Tècnics Catalans per al Progrés de l'Arquitecturs Contemporània – Group of Catalan Artists and Technicians for the Progress of Contemporary Architecture) as the Catalan section of the CIRPAC, the international body created to adress the "resolution of the problems" facing architecture at that moment in time. Illescas was one of the founders of the GATCPAC, and the Vilaró house is one of his most significant works, influenced by the characteristic "nautical" style of early rationalism.

The building stands on a steeply sloping site, obliging the architect to develop the programme for this private family residence over different levels, so that the structural elements assume a highly expressive role that is made apparent in the formal composition of the facades. The design of the openings, the handrails, the roof elements, are fully representative of the typological constants that were to define so much of the work of the GATCPAC.

Illescas designed the building at no. 96, c/ Padua (1934-1935), of which he himself was the owner, where not only the general aspects of the project but the handling of the interior finishing (lifts, stairs, floors, plinths, bathrooms and kitchens) reveals his concern to give function priority over form, simplifying this to the maximum without neglecting the design of each element, however secondary its importance might appear.

Illescas is also the architect of the Casa Mansana in the paseo de Sant Gervasi, nos. 1-3 (1935-1940).

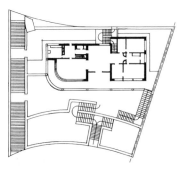

7
Unión y Fénix Español building   1927-1931

Paseo de Gràcia, 21
Eusebi Bona Puig, architect
Bus 7, 22, 24, 28. Metro L3 (Passeig de Gràcia)

The project adheres to a model established in advance by the client, an insurance company (founded in 1908), as regards the siting, the dynamic composition of the volumes and the monumental character, primarily influenced here by 19th-century French bourgeois and North American architecture rather than the local building tradition or the Art Nouveau and eclecticist resonances of the Barcelona Ensanche in which it so singularly distinguishes a corner site.

Bona adopted a semicircular form for the central volume of the building, an unusual treatment of the generally chamfered corner of the Ensanche block, and emphasized its monumental character with the order of paired Corinthian columns on the principal floors, topped by free-standing sculptures by

Frederic Marés, going on to crown the whole with a high-tamboured cupola surmounted by a bronze figure of the young Ganymede standing astride a phoenix with outstretched wings, symbol of eternal life, a sculptural group by Saint-Marceau. This volume houses the two main flights of stairs serving all parts of the building, which was inaugurated on March, 22nd of 1931.

Of particular interest within this same monumentalist language, which continued to be employed in Barcelona until the 50s, are a number of works by the architect Francesc Nebot Torrents, including the Coliseum cinema, the apartment buildings in c/ Balmes at nos. 297 and 301 (circa 1929), no. 303 (1944-1945), no. 360-366 and no. 363 (circa 1935), and the Schmith house (no. 368, 1946-1949).

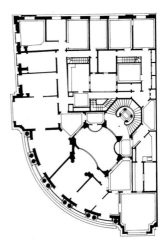

8
Casal Sant Jordi

C/ Casp, 24-26; c/ Pau Claris, 81
Francesc Folguera Grassi, architect
Bus 22, 24, 28, 39, 45, 47. Metro L1, L2, L4 (Urquinaona)

Belonging to the same line of formal expressionism as the Masana apartments, this building designed by Folguera is one of the outstanding achievements of 20th-century Catalan architecture, and was in its turn influenced by the innovative currents then stirring in Central Europe, but without moving too far from the classicist approach typical of the first *Noucentista* architecture.

The building's plurality of function, with the lower floors devoted to offices, the remainder to rented apartments, and the attic being occupied by the owner of the property, is apparent in the ordering and design of the openings, with void predominating over solid in the lower part, with this ratio being inverted as we move up the building. The owner's apartment on the attic floor is laid out over two levels, opening towards the interior of the block, onto a terrace-garden with a pond, the glass bottom of which serves as a skylight for the lower interior courtyard beneath. An external perimeter corridor filters out much of the noise from the street and acts as the distribution space for all the rooms of the house.

Presiding over the main facade is a sculpture of Saint George by Joan Rebull. The design of the pavings, the lift cage and shaft, the carpentry and metalwork and the ornamental details all reflect Folguera's sympathies with Art Déco.

The building was converted in 1989 to provide the new headquarters for the Generalitat de Catalunya's Ministry of Justice, under the direction of the architect Ignasi Sánchez Domènech.

Attic floor plan.

24

9
Apartment building

1930-1931

C/ Muntaner, 342-348
Josep Lluís Sert López, architect
Bus 58, 64. FF.CC. Generalitat (Muntaner)

Josep Lluís Sert and Josep Torres Clavé were the driving forces –by way of the GATCPAC– behind the introduction into Catalonia of the innovative architectonic and cultural movement that swept through Europe in the thirties. Torres Clavé was to die at the front in 1939, fighting in defence of the Republic, and Sert abandoned the country at the end of the Civil War, that same year, and settled in the United States, where he gained for himself a considerable international reputation. This series of circumstances has played its part in the subsequent mythologizing of the few works of Catalan rationalist architecture actually constructed; an architecture that for all its interest as a cultural phenomenon is of relatively modest significance in the wider European context of the time.

In this building, regarded as his first mature work within the GATCPAC and a classic of Catalan modernist culture, Sert utilizes the repertoire of concepts and forms habitually associated with the Modern Movement: duplex apartments with double-height interior spaces, studio flats on the attic level with terrace-gardens, a metal structure with plaster-rendered brickwork facades, balconies on the corners, and so on.

Sert also designed the building at c/ Rosselló no. 36 (1930) and the Joyería Roca jewellers' shop at no. 18, paseo de Gràcia (1934), on the site formerly occupied by the Café Torino, one of the most interesting and celebrated Modernista establishments in the city.

10
Apartment building   **1931**

Via Augusta, 61
German Rodríguez Arias, architect
Bus 16, 17, 22, 24, 28. FF.CC. Generalitat (Gràcia)

In this building, comprising ground floor and six upper floors on a gap site, Rodríguez Arias (also one of the founders of the GATCPAC) made a controversial break with established formal canons and incorporated a number of elements –some of them alien to orthodox rationalism– such as the variation in the rhythm of the openings or the zigzag arrangement of the attics.

In 1958, the architect himself reformed the ground floor and in 1963 extended and modified the top floor to excellent effect: a subtle frontage of metal pillars set flush with the facade manages, without altering the clearly apparent original volumetry, to lend unity to the composition as a whole.

Originally, the rendering of the main facade was of pink stucco, with the rear facade in white. In contrast, all of the component elements enclosing the building –the wood and metalwork of the windows, the tubular metal handrails, the fibre-reinforced concrete spandrels and the composition paving of the balconies– were grey in colour. These materials and colours, having suffered the ravages of time, were restored when the building was refurbished between 1988 and 1991 by the City Council under the direction of the architects Joan Rovira Casajuana and Bel Moretó Navarro.

The Astoria building, at nos. 193-197 c/ París (1933-1934), in which some authors have discerned the influence of Walter Gropius, is also –with the exception of the cinema salon– by Germán Rodríguez Arias.

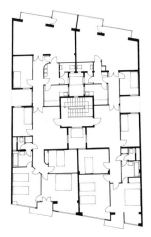

Plan of the 2nd, 3rd and 4th floors.

11
Casal del Metge

Via Laietana, 31
Adolf Florensa Ferrer and Enric Català Català, architects
Bus 16, 17, 19, 45. Metro L4 (Jaume I)

The major contribution in terms of new building made by Adolf Florensa –an acclaimed restorer of Barcelona monuments– is perhaps the introduction to the city of a language with its roots in Florentine civic classicism, which he developed with great skill and which endowed the newly constructed Via Laietana with a restrained and elegant monumentality, somewhat appeasing the irritation provoked by the impact of opening this avenue through the historic centre of the city. In this same street Florensa had already constructed, prior to his medical practitioners' headquarters, the Cambó house (no. 30, 1921-1925) and, a little later, the Fomento del Trabajo Nacional building (no. 34, 1931-1936, in collaboration with Josep Goday).

The facade of the Casal del Metge is divided into three orders: the lower, with its cushioned facing and round half-point arches; the central, with a rhythm of vertically proportioned windows diminishing in scale as we move up the facade, those on the principal floor being crowned with triangular pediments, and the upper, in the form of a loggia with Tuscan pilasters and columns under a cornice and central pediment. Of particular note in the interior are the central vestibule-courtyard, the stairway with its painted ceramic decoration, recalling the ornamentation of Barcelona's Faculty of Medicine in the Casa de Convalecencia, and the functions room. The first stone was laid on the 5th of March 1931, and the building was inaugurated on the 10th of December 1932.

12
Controlled-rent apartment building 1933
Av. de Gaudí, 56; c/ Castillejos (unnumbered)
Pere Benavent de Barberà Abelló, architect
Bus 19, 50. Metro L2 (Sagrada Família), L5 (Hospital de Sant Pau)

Benavent himself confessed that this building is a replica of the one by Josep Lluís Sert at no. 36, c/ Rosselló, although –in the architect's opinion– it "improves" the composition of the facade and the handling of the construction; an assertion that seems to be supported by the comparative study of the two buildings by professors of construction José Luis González and Albert Casals.

The building has a V-shaped plan, with facades on two streets not parallel to one another, and four apartments to a floor, two on either facade, opening to the exterior by way of their terraces. The structural system is based on load-bearing walls, while the exposed brickwork is bullnosed around the openings. The terraces, with their metal screen balustrades, owe much to the pronounced horizontality of the imposing floor slabs.

Benavent was concerned to find a new way of producing modern architecture free of the dictates of rationalist orthodoxy (of which he was highly critical), which was to place the emphasis on greater rationality in the construction rather than on innovation in the formal aspects, and this led him to distance himself from what he called Le Corbusier's "recipes" and to maintain his hold on the classicist spirit of Catalan *Noucentisme*. Other important buildings by Benavent from this period are: the Casa Esquerdo (c/ Balmes, 220, 1931-1932); the Cardona house (c/ París, 127, 1935-1940); the Casa J. Esteva, "la Punyalada", paseo de Gràcia, 104-108, 1935-1940) and the Casa Izquierdo (c/ Madrazo, 83-87, 1936).

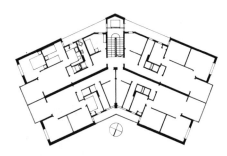

13
Casa Viladot

Av. de Gaudí, 71; c/ Castillejos, (unnumbered)
Jaume Mestres Fossas, architect
Bus 19, 50. Metro L2 (Sagrada Família), L5 (Hospital de Sant Pau)

Mestres Fossas is considered to be one of the key figures of Barcelona's architectural avant-garde of the second quarter of the 20th century. Although his work stands apart from orthodox rationalism (despite the fact that he became a member of the GATCPAC in 1931) and reveals evident resonances of *Noucentista* classicism, it manifests an openly progressive attitude.

The Viladot house, constructed on a pentagonal site with three street facades, is ordered on the basis of a rigidly symmetrical layout disposed around a central pentagonal stairwell. The facades, devoid of any overlaid ornamentation but making allusion to the graphic style of Art Déco, display a pronounced horizontality thanks to the continuous line of imposts framing the window openings. A comparable, although perhaps less successful, solution can be seen in the Casa Ginestà

(Av. de Gaudí, 44, 1931) by the same architect.

Also by Mestres are the Pabellón de Artistas Reunidos, from 1929 (since demolished, although the gates are conserved in the "Biosca & Botey" shop on the corner of c/ Còrsega and Rambla de Catalunya); the Seix y Barral publishing house, also demolished; the Sans houses (plaza Molina, 1-7, 1933-1934) and the Escola Blanquerna school (Instituto Menéndez Pelayo) at Via Augusta, 138-156, 1930-1933. In a late work, the Finanzauto building at c/ Balmes, 216-218, dating from 1954, Mestres incorporated a series of sculptural panels designed by Antoni Tàpies, alluding to the teaching the Piarists (the original proprietors of the building).

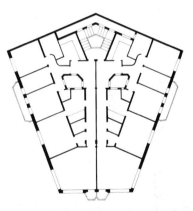

Reliefs by Antoni Tàpies (1954) on the Finanzauto building.

14
Collaso i Gil school complex 1932-1935

C/ de Sant Pau, 109 bis
Josep Goday Casals, architect
Bus 20, 64, 91. Metro L3 (Paral.lel)

Goday designed many of the new school buildings (Pere Vila, Milà i Fontanals, Ramon Llull) constructed by the city's reconvened municipal Commission for Culture between 1918 and 1922 but which, as a result of the imposition of the 1st Dictatorship in 1923, were not opened until 1931, under the 2nd Republic. The Collaso i Gil complex was designed fourteen years later, after the *Noucentista* fashion for evocations of cultured rural architecture that inspired these earlier school buildings had apparently exhausted itself. The change, however, was simply one of formal language, since the functional programmes and corresponding spatial solutions changed very little.

The building in c/ Sant Pau was named after the philanthropist Josep Collaso –who financed the operation to remedy the lack of schools in this working-class neighbourhood around the Romanesque church of Sant Pau del Camp– and comprises three volumes in a U-shaped layout with a courtyard in the middle. The semi-basement level contains the school's functions hall; the ground floor is given over to infants' classrooms, dining rooms and offices, and the next three floors to classrooms for older pupils, with the top floor, set back from the line of the facade, accommodating classrooms for art teaching.

The construction, whose formal inspiration comes from the contemporary Scandinavian architecture with which Goday was well acquainted, has exposed brickwork facades combining a tendency towards volumetric simplicity with a rich and varied exploitation of the different bonds and formal devices suggested by the use of brick.

15
Gardens in the Plaza Francesc Macià

1928-1934

Nicolás María Rubió Tudurí, architect

Bus 6, 7, 33, 34, 66

Rubió Tudurí, one of the most striking personalities of 20th-century Catalan culture, owed his introduction to landscape gardening to his work with J. C. Forestier on the preparations for the 1929 International Exhibition. As head of Barcelona City Council's parks and gardens service –a post he held for over twenty years– he created a series of gardens that must rank as one of the most interesting achievements of Catalan architecture during this period.

In contrast to the geometric gardens of the French tradition, Rubió reasserted the landscaped garden of Mediterranean tradition. The solution adopted for the central island of the plaza Francesc Macià marks the advent of this new conception of the city garden in Barcelona.

Rubió was also concerned to ensure that the landscaping would help to define the urban spaces and complement the architecture in whose midst it was situated. Outstanding examples of this are the Eduard Marquina gardens (Turó Park), dating from 1934 (featuring sculptures by E. Cerdan and Borrell Nicolau, amongst others), the gardens of the Palacio Real in Pedralbes (laid out in 1925), or the landscaped plaza in front of the Passion facade of Gaudí's Sagrada Familia.

The north side of the plaza Francesc Macià is delimited by two buildings with a monumental character, dating from the same period as the gardens themselves: the Ferrer-Cajigal apartment buildings at nos. 1-5 and 6, designed in 1928 by the architect Josep Rodríguez Lloveras, which adopt the curve of the circular plaza.

16
Casa Jaume Espona

1933-1935

C/ Camp d'en Vidal, 16; c/ Aribau, 243
Raimon Duran Reynals, architect
Bus 58, 64

Duran Reynals, a highly gifted architect whose importance transcends the bounds of any single language or school, was a member of the GATC-PAC, although he made no more than occasional use of the group's aesthetic postulates, and frequently at times when he was also working on projects whose formal characteristics are clearly at variance with the group's premisses. At the same time, in Duran Reynals' architecture the repertoire of rationalism was enrolled in the service of a composition whose roots are profoundly classicist, with the result that his work in the rationalist line is arguably that movement's most beautiful and elegant testimony in the city of Barcelona.

The work which best expresses Duran's engagement with orthodox rationalism, closer to Sert and Rodríguez Arias than the rest of his output of this period, is the house for Jaume Espona.

A house "without cornices or neoclassical mouldings" –in the words of Nicolás Rubió Tudurí– "but with an undeniable internal inspiration of serenity, of formal purity and harmony".

Other notable examples of this phase of Duran's work, more or less rationalist in tendency, are the Casa Francisca Espona at no. 368, c/ Muntaner (1932), the Barangé private residence at no. 22, c/ Monestir in Pedralbes (1932-1934) and the Casa Cardenal, c/ Roger de Llúria nos. 132-138 and c/ Còrsega no. 364 (1935), contemporary with and physically quite close to the Casa Espona described below, with its classicist stamp.

Casa Cardenal.

17
Casa Espona

1935

C/ Roger de Llúria, 124; c/ Rosselló, 281 bis
Raimon Duran Reynals, architect
Bus 20, 21, 39, 45, 47. Metro L3, L5 (Diagonal)

Contemporary with the neighbouring rationalist Casa Cardenal, this apartment building is perhaps the finest work of Duran's extensive production, and came to constitute the model for much of Barcelona's post-Civil War architecture.

The perfect composition of the facade (with its elegant use of elements of the classical tradition at key points – plinth, cornice, arrisses, windows; the balanced proportions of its solids and voids, and the chromatic effects of the brick and stone) reveals the extent to which Duran evolved his own highly personal strand of academicism, while the supremely accomplished internal distribution is accompanied by the optimum functioning and great atmospheric quality of the interior as a whole.

Other later works by Duran in the same line are the Dolors Marsans house, c/ Vico, 21 (1942), the recently demolished Casa Rosal, Via Augusta, 217-223 (1944), and the houses in the Av. Pedralbes, at nos. 58, 64 and 66 (1947-1949). Rubió Tudurí wrote the following with regard to the Marsans house: "The English architects of the Renaissance succeeded in bringing Latin forms to England... now Duran Reynals brings English forms to a Latin country. The outcome of this double adaptation is, in Duran's hands, admirable".

We should also mention here a number of residential buildings by other architects: those at c/ Francesc Pérez Cabrero, 5-9 (1944-1948), c/ Josep Bertrand, 11 (1946) and Via Augusta, 173 (1949), all by Francesc Mitjans; the building by F. J. Barba Corsini at passeig Bonanova, 105-107 (1949), and the Lacuna, house by Antoni Fisas, at c/ Valero, 12 (1949).

18
Casa Bloc

1932-1936

Paseo de Torras i Bages, 91-105
Josep Lluís Sert, Josep Torres Clavé and Joan B. Subirana, architects
Bus 35, 40, 73, 203. Metro L1 (Torras i Bages)

Together with the Dispensari Central Antituberculós, this workers' housing complex is one of the most representative instances of the GATCPAC's achievements, particularly significant in the light they shed on the relationship between the policy initiatives of the autonomous government of Catalonia during Spain's 2nd Republic and the innovative content of the proposals coming from the architectural avant-garde.

The Casa Bloc, with its 107 apartments, was commissioned by the Commissariat for Workers' Housing of the Generalitat de Catalunya as an alternative to the extended neighbourhood of detached houses. The plan in the form of a double U and the layout of the apartments over two floors recreate the theoretical postulates put forward by Le Corbusier for the Immeubles-villas.

In addition to high levels of hygiene and comfort (through ventilation from facade to facade, access corridor along the more shaded side of the block, where the bathrooms and kitchens are located, etc.), the apartments in the Casa Bloc were to enjoy a series of communal services and amenities such as a kindergarten, library, social club, sports facilities, and so on, the provision of which was prevented by the Civil War from 1936-1939. After the war the building was extended with the addition of a block of police housing.

Since 1985, the Diputació de Barcelona –the present proprietor– has been actively restoring the building and adapting it to meet present-day requirements of habitability, under the direction of the architect Jaume Sanmartí.

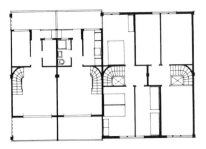

Typical floor plan.

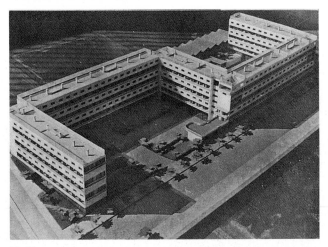

Model.

19
Dispensario antituberculoso　　　　　1934-1938

Pasaje Sant Bernat, 10; c/ Torres i Amat, (unnumbered)
Josep Lluís Sert, Josep Torres Clavé and Joan B. Subirana, architects
Bus 24, 41, 50, 54, 55, 64, 66. Metro L1, L2 (Universitat)

The dispensary was constructed within the fabric of the 5th district, the most densely populated and insalubrious in the city. The urbanistic thinking of the GATCPAC for these old central districts consisted of strategically vacating impoverished parts of the built fabric to let in air and light and alleviate their oppressive density of population. With commission from the City Council to design this building, the group felt encouraged to see this as a chance to put into practice their postulates with regard to the socialization of the hospital environment.

On an irregular plot, the two blocks containing the various medical facilities are disposed in an L-shaped plan, with the remaining space providing a garden and the roof accommodating sun terraces. The construction system differentiates between the metal structure and the partitions dividing the various spaces, and elements such as stairs, porticoes, the plinth on the ground floor, etc., in the same way that the different parts of the building are differentiated and articulated on the basis of their function.

Between 1982 and 1992, the building was restored by the Department of Health and Social Security of the Generalitat de Catalunya under the direction of the architects Mario Corea, Francisco Gallardo, Raimon Torres and Edgardo Manino. A number of obsolete elements were replaced, and new features in line with modern concepts of comfort introduced. The building is today a health centre, the Centro de Atención Primaria Dr. Lluís Sayé.

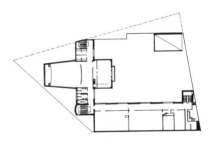

20
Parish church of Santa Teresa del Nen Jesús

1932-1940

Via Augusta, 72
Josep Domènech Mansana, architect
Bus 16, 17, 22, 24, 28. FF.CC. Generalitat (Gràcia)

Domènech Mansana was the son of the architect Domènech Estapà, who produced a series of outstanding works which rank amongst the finest eclectic architecture of 19th- and 20th-century Barcelona, some of which –such as the Carmelite convent in the Av. Diagonal– were completed by the son. Domènech Mansana's own prolific body of work (much of it commissioned by the public authorities) is of notable quality, and in stylictic terms faithfully reflects its time — from mediaeval historicism and *Modernisme* through to the formulas of popular architecture sponsored by *Noucentisme.*

In 1932 he drew up the project for the new parish church of Santa Teresa, whose construction was interrupted, with the walls rising to a height of four metres, by the Civil War of 1936-1939. Construction of the building was completed in 1940, although various aspects of the finishing and fitting out continued until until the sixties, and it was late in that decade before the adjoining rectory was completed.

The facade, of great expressive force, and entirely faced with sandstone in two tones, has as its compositional axis the great belltower, rising up on the plane of the facade itself, and the main door with its semicircular arch and sequence of archivolts. The exterior of the building presents echoes of Nordic architecture, especially that of the Finn Eliel Saarinen and the Dane Jensen Klint. However, the decoration of the three naves in the interior is more conventional in conception, essentially neoclassical in style.

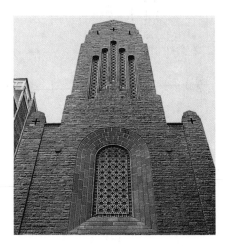

21
Apartment building

1934-1940

Av. de la Diagonal, 419-421; c/ Enric Granados, 126
Ricardo de Churruca Dotres, architect
Bus 6, 7, 15, 27, 30, 33, 34

Churruca was one of the founders of the GATCPAC, acting as librarian to the group together with Rodríguez Arias, who also shared in the direction of this block of apartments on the Avinguda Diagonal.

The volumetric conception and the formal treatment given to the facades clearly evidences the expressionist tendency cultivated by Churruca within his far from orthodox rationalism. Each facade follows a different compositional scheme, situating the volumes of the projecting terraces on different axes (only the terraces on the chamfered corner of c/ Enric Granados maintains a criterion of symmetry), but with an overall unity to which the uniform rendering of the facings makes a significant contribution. The scheme as a whole is handled as a series of inde-pendent blocks of apartments, conforming to the urban layout of the Ensanche and, without breaking with the existing alignment, opens on one side to connect the interior of the block with the street.

Churruca also designed the Casa Conill, at no. 3, c/ Iradier (1935). Of the series of buildings constructed in these years by architects whom, in the words of Oriol Bohigas, we might describe as "fringe rationalists" (with regard to their having distanced themselves from the orthodox GATCPAC line), we should note in particular the Estradé house at c/ Santaló, 70 (1926); the Vilà de la Riva house at c/ Balmes, 392-396, by Josep M. Sagnier Vidal (1935-1942), and the Ballvé house at no. 166 of the same street, by Ricard Ribas Seva (1934-1936).

22
Clínica Barraquer

1934-1940

C/ Laforja, 88; c/ Muntaner, 314
Joaquim Lloret Homs, architect
Joaquim Barraquer, ophthalmologist
Bus 58, 64. Metro FF.CC. Generalitat (Muntaner)

In order to understand the original exterior aspect of this surprising building, it is necessary to imagine it as having only a ground floor and three upper floors (the top floor comprising two wings set back on either side of a circular volume at a tangent to the alignment of the chamfered corner and surmounted by an imposing cornice). It is also necessary to spirit away the superimposed pillars which run vertically the full height of the facade and cut across the originally continuous horizontal openings, a clumsy modification introduced with the construction of additional floors in the sixties.

In spite of this unfortunate reform (the desired extension could have been handled with greater sensitivity, but by that time Professor Barraquer had died), the building has preserved its indisputable spatial values and its great charm, thanks to its outstanding design and the perfect harmony between architecture, ornamentation and furnishings achieved by its architect and ophthalmologist – who together worked on the basic scheme and many of the details.

The decorative elements in the public rooms, as well as the design of doors, stairs and light fittings, are clear –if tardy– references to the iconography of Art Déco.

In subsequent works the architect Lloret moved towards monumentalist eclecticism, and it is in this light that we should regard the F.S. house at no. 462, c/ Muntaner, and the "Rancho Grande" complex at Via Augusta, 170-180 (1940-1944).

The facade before being reformed in the sixties.

23
Fàbregas building
(Urquinaona skyscraper) **1935-1944**

C/ de les Jonqueres, 18; c/ Trafalgar; plaza Urquinaona
Luis Gutiérrez Soto (project) and
Carlos Martínez Sánchez (site supervision), architects
Bus 16, 17, 19, 39, 41, 42, 45, 47, 55. Metro L1, L2, L4 (Urquinaona)

The Madrid architect Gutiérrez Soto constructed the major part of his work in his native city. Between 1928 and 1939 –during which time he designed his one Barcelona building– cultivated, within his generally eclectic approach, the language of rationalism. After the Civil War he moved, in his public buildings, towards an El Escorial-style academicism (as in his 1948 Ministerio del Aire, ironically dubbed "the monastery of the Air") and, in his residential architecture, towards a more personal vision, of notable quality, although now quite distant from the modern language he employed with such skill in the project for the Fàbregas building.

Construction of this first Barcelona "skyscraper", with its 15 floors of offices (the first five) and apartments, commenced in 1936, shortly after the outbreak of the Civil War, and for this reason it was not completed until 1944.

In conformity with the shape of the plot, the building was conceived as three volumes, one of them curving, around a triangular courtyard at the vertices of which are the vertical communications and into which the toilets and other services ventilate. On the exterior, a projecting volume with a curving axis accommodating a series of terraces constitutes the building's most expressive formal feature, at the point at which this overlooks the plaza.

Carlos Martínez designed another interesting apartment building executed in terms of an essentially rationalist language, at Via Augusta, 12 (1932).

24
Cía. Anònima de Filatures
Fabra & Coats building   **1941-1944**

C/ Bruc, 50; Gran Via de les Corts Catalanes, 676
Raimon Duran Reynals, architect

Bus 7, 18, 45, 47, 56

After the Civil War Duran continued to pursue the academicist line initiated with the Casa Espona, designing a series of buildings whose commercial character led him to incorporate elements drawn from American eclectic architecture, but retaining at all times that freedom in the composition which gives his classicism its own highly personal stamp. In these buildings, almost all with facades of white artificial stone, there is a predominant verticality in the ordering of the openings, strengthened by the presence of full-height pilasters or projections, and at the same time a retention of the classical division into three horizontal bands marked by and imposts and cornices.

The Fabra & Coats building, the one for the Cía. Anónima de Actividades Varias (c/ Marià Cubí, 10-22, 1950), the Casa Mercè Imbern de Cardenal (c/ Ferran Agulló, 10, 1945), the Torre Muñoz (paseo de Gràcia, 105, 1949-1952) and the Casa Damians (c/ Balmes, 96, 1954) all manifest not only Duran's great qualities as a designer but his professionalism in the field of construction.

Between 1939 and 1949, Duran worked on the María Reina church (carretera d'Esplugues, 103), begun in the 20s by Rubió Tudurí. He designed the bell tower, with its markedly Renaissance character, the baldachin and the chapel of the Most Holy.

The architect Francesc Mitjans, a follower of Duran in all his academicist lines, also provided his own response to the works mentioned above: the buildings at c/ Balmes, 182 (1945-1948) and Ronda de General Mitre, 140 (1947-1949).

Bell tower of the María Reina church.

40

25
Apartment building

1941-1943

C/ Amigó, 76
Francesc Mitjans Miró, architect
Bus 14. FF.CC. Generalitat (Muntaner)

This is an extraordinary building –in view of its social context, the novelty for the city of the solutions it put forward, and its subsequent influence– which can be considered as one of the pioneers of a new phase in Catalan architecture, in contact once again, in spite of its political isolation, with the European avant-gardes. On account of its chronology, however, and perhaps the absence of any expressly modern intention (the work is, in the architect's own words, "more 'spontaneous' than modern"), it asks to be analyzed in the present section of this study.

The architect Mitjans, who was at the same time producing works whose formal affinities were with the classicism of Duran Reynals, was to arrive at very different solutions suggested by

his reflections on another of the basic aspects of Duran's architecture: the fitness of the plan. In breaking away from the typical apartment layout of the Ensanche (which would not have served here), he was looking for "a more functional plan", with the introduction of the continuous terrace for the first time in a residential building in Barcelona. However, in the interiors (vestibule, stairs, carpentry and decorative detailing) the apartments retain all the weight of academicist tradition.

In this same line, Mitjans went on to design the apartments at Mandrí, 2-6 (1950-1952), at Vallmajor, 26-28 on the corner of c/ Freixa, 37 (1952-1954), and the clinic for Dr Soler Roig at c/ Vallmajor, 25 (1952-1954, extended in 1991).

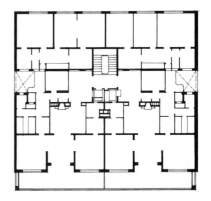

26
Banco Vitalicio de España 1942-1950

Paseo de Gràcia, 11; Gran Via de les Corts Catalanes, 632
Lluís Bonet Garí, architect
Bus 7, 22, 24, 28. Metro L1, L2, L3 (Catalunya)

Lluís Bonet Garí, a follower of Gaudí who worked in his studio in the Sagrada Familia, was one of the those who after the great architect's death strove to keep alive various aspects of Gaudí's legacy. Bonet's civil and residential work is, however, far removed from Gaudí's aesthetic principles, and much closer to classicist eclecticisms, handled with measured monumentality to reveal a mastery of construction and a fine formal sensibility.

This is the case with the Banco Vitalicio de España building, composed of four independently structured volumes (of reinforced concrete, in order, as the project report says, "to give the building a homogeneous complexion from foundations to crown"), consisting of three groups of apartments and offices and a theatre, in the interior of the block, with access by way of a shopping gallery which occupies the whole of the ground floor and receives daylight from a small landscaped courtyard.

The facades are constructed of a double skin of brick, the outer layer faced with Galician granite on the ground floor and sandstone from Montjuïc for the remainder. The central volume on the chamfered corner, which becomes successively smaller as it ascends, rises to a height of 75 metres.

Other works by Bonet Garí include the Casa Patxot (c/ Monestir, 12, 1942) and the Instituto Nacional de Previsión (Gran Via de les Corts Catalanes, 587, c/ Balmes, 20), designed in 1947.

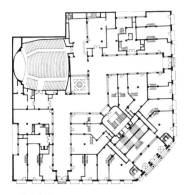

27
Bloque CLIP

1949-1952

C/ Còrsega, 571-597; c/ Lepant, 334-348;
c/ Indústria, 122-136; c/ Padilla, 301-317
Raimon Duran Reynals, architect
Bus 15, 19, 20, 45, 47, 50

The building occupies an entire city block in the sector of the Ensanche diagonally traversed by the av. Gaudí (running from the Sagrada Familia to the Hospital de Sant Pau), constructed when the area was beginning to establish itself as a residential neighbourhood. This closed, unitary city block, with its compact volumetry and central courtyard, in the fashion of a simultaneous grouping of adjoining residential units enveloped by a common facade evidencing the absence of direct continuity between them.

Each residential block has four apartments to a floor, two opening onto the street facade and two onto the central courtyard. In either case the lounge/dining room and main bedroom open onto the exterior, while the other rooms are ventilated by small, dark wells corresponding to the stairs and service courtyards.

This exceptional building-cum-city block (in the design of which the architects Raimon Duran and Antoni Fisas played a part) marks a point of inflexion in the evolution of residential architecture in Barcelona. In urbanistic terms this constitutes the final flourishing of an already outmoded conception (construction of the block of c/ Escorial was then just beginning). In formal terms, the academic language, ably but by now rhetorically employed, announces the demise of an exhausted formula.

A similar and contemporaneous development, utilizing a more innovative approach to the form of the city block, is the apartment building constructed by the Caixa de Pensions at c/ Andrade, 155-175 and c/ Concili de Trento, designed by Manuel Cases Lamolla (1950-1954).

Apartments at c/ Andrade, 155-175.

28
Parish church of
La Mare de Déu dels Àngels   1942-1957

C/ Balmes, 78; c/ València, 244
Josep Danés Torras, architect
Bus 7, 16, 17

In 1936, at the outbreak of the Civil War, many of Barcelona's churches were destroyed or damaged. After the war, the newly installed regime provided the impetus for a major programme of church reconstruction and new building, clearly reflecting the diversity of architectonic criteria of the *Noucentista* period.

Some of the new constructions followed –more or less literally– the Florentine tradition introduced by Rubió Tudurí and other *Noucentista* Catalan architects of the pre-war years. This can be seen in the Perpetu Socor church by Joaquim Porqueras Bañeres (c/ Balmes, 98, 1950); the Sant Miquel dels Sants church by Antoni Fisas (c/ Escorial, 163, 1950-1963) and the Montserrat church, an annexe of the Sarrià Capuchin monastery by Pere Benavent de Barberà (1936-1962).

Although conceived in very similar typological terms, the Mare de Déu dels Àngels church, standing on a chamfered Ensanche corner, seeks to reinstate other languages of the pre-war years more related to avant-garde movements, and clearly reveals influences drawn from Déco and northern European architecture, especially on the main facade, with the incorporation of large upright windows, and above all in the bell tower, built of stone.

Josep Danés was also responsible for the reconstruction of the Santa Maria de la Bonanova church (plaza de la Bonanova, 12-14, 1940-1950), which draws its inspiration from the form of the early Christian basilica.

1951-1977

More than a decade after the end of the Spanish Civil War, and a little over five years after the conclusion of the Second World War, the first stirrings of a renovation in architecture began to be felt in Catalonia. The old schemes and languages no longer held any attraction for the new generations of professionals, and were to soon to be discarded by developers and constructors. The first achievements of the hesitant progress towards an autonomous construction industry made it possible to adopt new approaches to design. The result was an architecture of dignity and efficiency, with a diversity of languages, and characterized by a reasoned balancing of creativity, adaptability to available technical and economic resources and validity in the resolution of objectives.

The starting point of this renovation is located by the critical establishment in the so-called "Grup R" which came into being soon after the Catalan architects recovered, for the first time since the Civil War, the spirit of debate and cooperation, thanks largely to the competition organized by the Colegio de Arquitectos de Cataluña y Baleares to tackle Barcelona's housing problem. On the 21st of August, 1951 –in the studio of the architects José Antonio Coderch and Manuel Valls, with Oriol Bohigas, Joaquim Gili, Josep Martorell, Josep Pratmarsó, Josep M. Sostres and Antoni de Moragas in attendance– the group's first management committee was constituted, defining as its primary purpose "the study of the problems of contemporary art and especially of architecture", with the aim of helping the country find its way out of the disorientation in which it languished, excluded as it was from the spirit of reconstruction abroad in Europe.

Over the course of a decade, the group's activities were uneven in many ways, but effective, and when it was disbanded, the group had an influential hand in the diversification of conceptual and formal tendencies: "Unlike the GATCPAC", Antoni de Moragas observed in an article in Serra d'Or in 1961, "Grup R lacked unity. Each one chose his own style...". Perhaps it also lacked someone to take a clear lead. José Antonio Coderch de Sentmenat might have exercised this function, but his sympathies with the regime in power raised a barrier between him and some of his colleagues and the critics that proved insuperable, and it was not long before he withdrew from the group. Oriol Bohigas –who was to emerge as one of the most attractive and contradictory figures in the Catalan culture of the second half of the century– was at the time still perhaps too young, perhaps too combative, to take on this unifying role.

The architecture of the fifties
But the "architecture of the fifties" (the best definition to date of the whole range of these unclassifiable architectures) was not the exclusive domain of the avant-gardes, and still less of any one group. It was a much wider phenomenon, manifested as much in private-sector housing and industry as in public building. Many instances of these, however, on account of the association –real or merely imputed– of their architects or promoters with the regime in power, have not until recently received the attention they rightly deserve. One example is the unjustified delay in appreciating the altar constructed in the Plaça Pius XII for the International Eucharistic Congress in 1952; another the work of Manuel Baldrich, architect of the Hogares Mundet church, one of the masterpieces of its quarter century.

The end of the Franco autarchy altered the panorama of architecture in Catalonia. The uncontrolled development of Spain in the sixties –responsible for so many disastrous interventions in the historic city centres and the malformation of the peripheral suburbs– spawned a poor architecture whose only criterion was maximum profits, and which plagued Barcelona to a special degree on account of the city's leading place in that process of economic expansion. This phenomenon attracted the participation of many of the architects –whether blessed with the benefits of power or not– who in the previous decade had contributed to the rebirth of architecture, and thus left the maintenance of an acceptable level of dignity to the care of an aware and conscientious minority.

Such a situation favoured the evolution within this minority of a more radical approach –also found in other European cultures of the time and in Grup R itself– not only towards architecture as a discipline in itself, but even to its role as catalyst of social change. Oriol Bohigas' 1957 text *Elogio de la Barraca* (In praise of the hut), denouncing official controlled-rent housing programmes that do nothing but institute the social and urban segregation of incoming migrants and those published shortly after it –*Elogi del totxo* (In praise of brick) and *Cap a una arquitectura realista* (Towards a realist architecture)– clearly announce this radicalization.

Catalan Realisme, that local reflection of a feeling especially identified with Italy, now posited itself as a belligerent theoretical position, as an act of ethical protest by architecture, which thus assumed a social role beyond that of its genuine field of action, and even as a formal current in the call for a return to architecture's traditional craft values, rejecting the illusory Utopia of an industrialized society.

One paradox in this realism is the fact that its heavyweight figures –champions of a "respect for the authentic processes of construction"– were within a few years to become the individuals who saw to it that the teaching in the Escuela de Arquitectura de Barcelona took the "project design" path, as an abstract exercise quite divorced from any understanding of construction, with the dire consequences this was to have for the Catalan architecture of the last quarter of the 20th century. Was realism not, in fact, a refusal to engage with the evolution of the science of buildings and structures after the Second World War and a taking refuge in a "traditional construction process" that was never properly understood?

At the opposite pole from realism in terms of formal currents, the most significant work in the Barcelona of those years was that of Josep Maria Fargas and Enric Tous, actively committed to providing local architectural culture with all the advantages of technology. Although their buildings had to

Altar for the International Eucharistic Congress. 1952. Josep Soteras Maurí.

Casa de la Marina. 1954. J. A. Coderch de Sentmenat (interior of show flat).

content themselves with being the products not of a real industrialization but of a skilled craft imitation of language of technology, the results are of great interest.

The mid-sixties brought Catalonia, and in particular Barcelona, into closer contact with Milanese Neo-Liberty in the context of a concern with integrating architecture into its urban setting. The principal exponent of this Italian influence on the Catalan architecture of the sixties was Federico Correa, a disciple of Coderch, whose personality is fundamental to any appreciation of the character of the period and its subsequent influence. Correa, as composition tutor at the Barcelona School of Architecture, promoted a very particular understanding of the relationships between form, function and "setting" –a relation latent in his own work– that was to shape an entire generation of Catalan architects.

As a consequence of these influences and a collective concern with control of the project as a means of ensuring "the quality of each point in the work" within the utilization of a limited formal repertoire, the schemes produced in the offices of Correa, of Bohigas and of certain of their former students and assistants manifested a proximity of approach that served as the basis for the so-called "Barcelona School". The "School" is not easily defined, since its constituent common principles extended to the rethinking of architecture's role in the new socio-economic context following its entry into crisis, and even to the social ideas and attitudes of its members (the only apparent contact, indeed, between these architects and the group of filmmakers also known as the "Barcelona School").

Two of the youngest participants in that "School", Oscar Tusquets and Lluis Clotet, were soon to introduce a new air into Catalan architecture. Their Casa Fullà (1967-1971), the contemporary Casa Penina in Cardedeu and, to an even greater extent, the Regàs de Llofriu house in the Empordà (1971-1972) represent a break "from within" with the architectonic culture that emerged with Grup R and affected their generation by way of the "Barcelona School". And once again this break was not confined to the definition of architecture, but also concerned the

social role of the architect. A number of architects had already found a sanctuary in the laxity of the "gauche divine", and there was a general move towards a relaxing of social commitment and a taking refuge in the vicious circle of design, yet another foretaste of what was in store for Barcelonese architecture in the final quarter of the 20th century.

The other history
But alongside this history of the discipline, which follows the thread of those movements and tendencies recognized

Casa de la Meridiana. 1959-1966. O. Bohigas, J. Martorell, D. Mackay.

ESADE building (model). Federico Correa Ruiz.

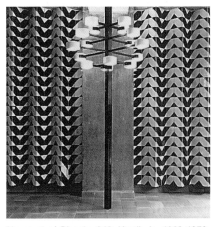

House at c/ Biscaia, 340. Vestibule. 1969-1970. Antoni de Moragas.

47

by the critics –very often at once judge and judged– as significant, there is a need for other parallel readings if we are to arrive at an understanding of the overall evolution of architecture in Barcelona during the period that concerns us here. We need to analyze various phenomena of importance for the city, some of them pushed to one side because of the circumstances of their promotion and construction or simply because the results proved difficult to reconcile with that ineffable concept, "cultured architecture". By way of example, the work of the Nuñez y Na-

Nuñez y Navarro apartment building. C/ Calábria, 162-164. 1959-1960.

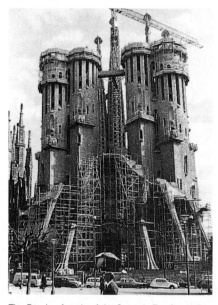

The Passion facade of the Sagrada Família. L. Bo-net Garí and I. Puig Boada. Work in progress in March 1972.

varro construction company is of interest not only for the impact on the urban landscape of its very extensive series of developments, but in sociological and construction terms.

The evident commercial success of the Nuñez company, coinciding with what has been seen as a shadowy period of in the political history of the city, and the indisputable fact that a number of its buildings were constructed on sites occupied by fine examples of Modernista architecture, some of which were demolished (such as the Trinxet house by Puig Cadafalch), effectively consigned this phenomenal factor in Barcelona's urban architecture to systematic rejection and neglect, so that it has never received the critical attention it merits.

Nor must we forget that throughout these twenty-five years, work was in progress on the Sagrada Família (what city would attempt to write its architectural history without mentioning its cathedral?), or fail to note the urban impact of sustained growth: those supposedly "singular" buildings which in the course of a few years permanently transformed the city, or the major public works (traffic intersections, underpasses, etc.), the quality of whose design is in not a few cases exceptional.

Incorporating some of these phenomena, and assigning others an appropriate place for the analysis they deserve, the text that follows presents in proper chronological order the most significant Barcelonese architecture of the third quarter of the 20th century.

29
Hotel Park

1950-1954

Av. Marquès de l'Argentera, 11
Antoni de Moragas Gallissà and
Francesc de Riba Salas, architects
Bus 14, 39, 40, 51. Metro L4 (Barceloneta)

The process of designing and constructing the Hotel Park coincided with Antoni de Moragas's own personal discovery of the Modern Movement. Throughout his life this cultured and public-spirited architect combined his work in architecture with an effective involvement in the affairs of his country.

In 1949, Moragas drew up a first scheme –"more or less eclectic in style", as his son Antoni recalls– which he then modified in two subsequent projects (1950 and 1951) after coming into contact with Bruno Zevi, Gio Ponti and Alvar Aalto on their respective visits to Barcelona.

While the Hotel Park makes palpable reference to Italian organicism in its break away from the traditional unitary conception of the facade, with the deconstruction of the planes and emphasizing of the structural elements, in other contemporaneous schemes (re-garded by some authorities as the first emergence of modern post-war architecture in Barcelona) such as the Fémina cinema (c/ Diputació, 259-261, 1951-1953, destroyed by fire in April 1991), there is an evident proximity to Alvar Aalto, the architect who most strongly influenced Moragas.

The hotel was restored in 1990 under the direction of Antoni de Moragas Spa, Moragas Gallissà's son, and Irene Sánchez. The work was carried out on the basis of the 1950 plans, introducing only the most essential adaptations, and restoring the original colours on the facades.

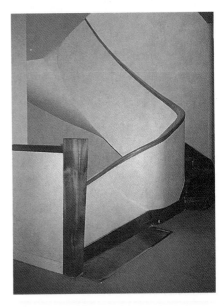

Casa de la Marina 1951-1954

Paseo Joan de Borbó, 43 (formerly Paseo Nacional)
José Antonio Coderch de Sentmenat and
Manuel Valls Vergès, architects
Bus 17, 39, 45, 47, 59, 64. Metro L4 (Barceloneta)

The work of José Antonio Coderch constitutes the most solidly coherent body of modern post-war Catalan architecture, in its commitment to recovering the values (constructive, spatial, formal and atmospheric) of vernacular architecture consecrated by tradition while at the same time incorporating the postulates of the Modern Movement.

This commitment is clearly expressed in the Casa de la Marina, one of the first manifestations of modernity –alongside the Hotel Park and the Cine Fémina by Antoni de Moragas– in the lethargic architectural panorama of those difficult years. The programme for small, publicly financed apartments presented a number of problems on account the nature of the plot; problems which were resolved by the intelligent and somewhat unconventional floor plan. The treatment of the exterior makes skillful use of the imposing and attractive alternation between ceramic facings and wooden blinds.

The building, which had been poorly maintained over the years, with the loss of various elements, including the crown of the facade, that had played an essential part in the reading of the original design, was restored during 1991-1992 under the control of the architects Gustavo Coderch, Carles Fochs and Jaume Avellaneda.

The Cooperativa Obrera la Maquinista residential block, on c/ Marquès de la Mina and c/ Maquinista, constructed between 1951 and 1953, and also in the Barceloneta district, is another example of the work of José Antonio Coderch.

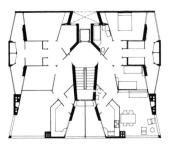

31
Apartment building

1954-1955

Av. de Pedralbes, 63
Raimon Duran Reynals, architect
Bus 22, 64, 75. FF. CC. Generalitat (Reina Elisenda)

With this building, which was commissioned by the Elisenda property company in July 1954, Duran returned to the legacy of the Modern Movement, without abandoning the classicist sensibility that is a constant presence in his work, adapted here to the new formal tendencies then gaining ground in the city.

The functional organization of the plan, with each floor accommodating two very large apartments, is also adapted to the new demands then being made by the middle classes on this type of free-standing block. As a result, the accesses and services are grouped together in a central core situated on the building's axis of symmetry, and the living areas and bedrooms –all of which open to the exterior, either directly or by way of ample continuous terraces with moveable blinds– are laid out around the perimeter. The planes of the facade have been fractured (the corners recessed in and the central stretches set back to make way for the terraces), so that the volume ac-quires greater movement and formal expressiveness.

Other outstanding examples of Duran's work from this period are the Casa Muntadas, at c/ Saragossa, 84 (1952), and the apartment building at Av. del Paral.lel, 87-89 (1962).

Also in the Av. de Pedralbes, at nos. 59-61, Francesc Mitjans constructed in 1957 a block of apartments which bears certain similarities to those by Duran, and which also evidences this same search for a new residential style for the upper middle classes.

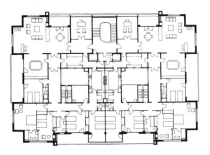

Congrés Eucarístic apartments   **1952-1961**

Plaza del Congrés Eucarístic; c/ Felip II
Carles Marquès Maristany, Antoni Pineda Gualba and
Josep Soteras Mauri, architects ·

Bus 18, 71. Metro L5 (Congrés)

The celebration in Barcelona of the 35th International Eucharistic Conference in 1952 was one of the occasions taken by the city in the course of the present century to impose some order on its growth and conclude various public works. One of the most important results was the series of subsidised apartment buildings sponsored by the bishop, Gregorio Modrego, to alleviate the acute housing shortage at a time when Barcelona was experiencing a very considerable influx of population.

On May 30th, 1952, the first 4 hectares of land was acquired, and in a short space of time this figure was more than quadrupled to arrive at the total of 16.5 hectares which was to provide the site for this city in miniature of 2,700 apartments, with shops, schools, churches and sports facilities, laid out in a combination of open and closed types of block, constituting one of the most important urban operations carried out in the city of Barcelona during the years of the 2nd Dictatorship.

It could be argued that the formal outcome is not entirely convincing, but the urbanistic and social factors must also be taken into account. The process adopted to select the future residents and distribute them within the development on the basis of type and size of family, occupation and geographical origin, together with the simultaneous construction of housing and provison of services and amenities, meant that the new neighbourhood could soon boast levels of civic and cultural activity rarely attained in the housing developments constructed in subsequent decades.

Plan of the neighbourhood.

Typical floor plan of one of the towers

33
Escorial residential group   **1952-1962**

C/ de l'Escorial, 50; c/ de la Legalitat
Josep Alemany Juvé, Oriol Bohigas Guardiola,
Josep Martorell Codina, Francesc Mitjans Miró,
Josep M. Ribas Casas and Manuel Ribas Piera, architects
Bus 21, 39. Metro L4 (Joanic)

The layout of the apartments in free-standing blocks with a relatively shallow depth available for construction, resulting in the elimination of the traditional interior courtyards, made it possible to provide extensive communal spaces –equipped with a variety of services and landscaped areas for leisure use– which connect directly with the surrounding streets, yet without these losing their urban character or suffering major distortions, thanks to the siting of the two perimeter blocks, similar in height to the neighbouring buildings, along the original street alignment.

Slightly stepped back from the line of c/ Escorial, which is broader than the other streets bounding the complex, is the cuboid tower block in exposed concrete and white tiling. In general conception (apartments laid out over two levels, horizontal communications galleries, isolated nuclei for vertical communications and services, etc.) this tower, presiding over and dignifying the residential group, reinstates many of the typological paradigms of the Modern Movement that had fallen out of view in post-war Barcelona.

The rationality and beauty of the ordering and the great architectonic quality of the apartment buildings make this complex one of the most interesting works of its period.

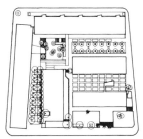

General plan of the complex.

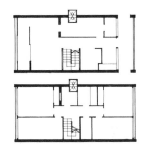

Typical floor plan of a duplex apartment.

Palacio Municipal de Deportes   1953-1955

C/ de la Guàrdia Urbana (formerly de la Tècnica), (unnumbered);
c/ Lleida, 40
Josep Soteras Mauri, Lorenzo García-Barbón and
Fernández de Henestrosa, architects; Frederic Folch, engineer
Bus 55, 57. Metro L1, L3 (Espanya)

This sports pavilion seating 10,000 spectators, constructed on the occasion of the II Mediterranean Games in Barcelona, and inaugurated on July 18th, 1955, provides an instance of that architecture which the critics almost totally ignored for many years – perhaps because it was promoted and built by the public authorities under the Dictatorship, perhaps because its aesthetic parameters do not correspond closely enough to the postulates of the avantgarde.

This is the most significant example of a moderated brutalism and an architecture laden with conscious contradictions: the structure is exposed, but converted into ornament or partially finished with autonomous lengths of glazed facade; the elements in tension terminate in evidently distended rounded forms, and the exposed concrete is concealed in places under unashamedly decorative stone cladding.

One remarkable element in this sports pavilion is the structure, consisting of eight arches of three-way articulated reinforced concrete with a double T section, produced on site and raised into position, parallel to the main facade. These arches, with a span of 65 metres, are partially hidden by the concrete and wooden plates of the ceiling, creating a sensation of extreme slenderness.

In 1957, Soteras designed the Luminor office building at plaza de Castella, 1-4.

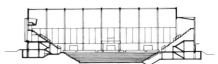

35
Futbol Club Barcelona Stadium   **1954-1957**

Travessera de les Corts, (unnumbered); av. Joan XXIII
Lorenzo García-Barbón, Francesc Mitjans Miró and
Josep Soteras Mauri, architects
Bus 15, 43, 54, 75. Metro L5 (Collblanc)

This is more than a stadium. It was opened on September 24th, 1957, and since then –given the social and civic role which F.C. Barcelona, owner of the stadium and itself described as "much more than a club", has always exercised– its significance for the community extends well beyond the bounds of its strictly sporting function. Its construction –which made use of technical resources never before employed in the city– represents the first collective act of Catalan self-affirmation after the Civil War, made tangible through architecture.

The original stadium had capacity for 90,000 spectators, almost half seated, and was constructed of reinforced concrete, with a number of interesting structural solutions which made for highly expressive facades, some of them featuring quite spectacular ramps of relative functional utility, intended to emphasize the modern character to which the club aspired. The roof covering the main stand –projecting out 40 metres over the terracing– is a parti-

cularly apt design, although the structural solution finally adopted is less attractive than the original concept, based on a system of braced cables.

On the occasion of the 1982 FIFA World Cup, the stadium was extended, bringing its capacity to almost 120,000 spectators, but entailing negative consequences for the architecture of the facades. In addition to Mitjans and Soteras, the architects Joan Pau Mitjans Perelló, Francesc Cavaller Soteras and Antoni Bergnes de las Casas worked on the extension.

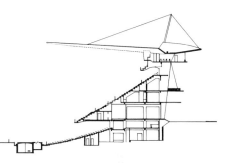

Hogares Ana G. de Mundet

1954-1957

Paseo de la Vall d'Hebron, (unnumbered)
Manuel Baldrich Tibau, architect
Bus 27, 73, 76, 85. Metro L3 (Montbau)

In 1927 the Diputació de Barcelona started to construct a building designed by Joan Rubió Bellver on this site, intended as a replacement for the Casa de la Caritad in the Raval district. Work was suspended for financial reasons with only a third of the building completed. In 1953, the architect Manuel Baldrich proposed to the corporation the construction of a residential and welfare complex for 3,000 people, an initiative made posible thanks to the major donation for charitable works made by Artur Mundet.

The topography of the site called for great care in the disposition of the buildings to ensure the creation of interesting exterior sequences and spaces. The communal services, the church and the functions hall occupy the geometrical axis of the complex and constitute the "community centre" of the new welfare housing development. The group of buildings for the elderly and the one occupied by junior schools are situated in different areas.

The church is the most interesting element here, a work of fundamental significance for the Catalan architecture of this period. Baldrich reworked models drawn from Nordic architecture, particularly that of Alvar Aalto, not only in terms of its spatial and construction qualities, but also in the design of the complementary elements and furniture. The church contains sculptures by J. M. Subirachs and Eudald Serra, paintings by Joan J. Tharrats, and stained glass by Jordi Domènech and Will Faber.

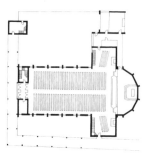

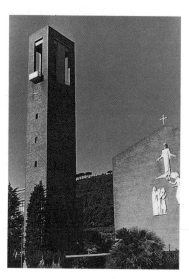

37
Apartment building

1957

C/ Sant Antoni Maria Claret, 318-332
Antoni de Moragas Gallisà and
Francesc de Riba Salas, architects
Bus 15, 19, 20, 45, 47, 50. Metro L5 (Camp de l'Arpa)

This building initiated a phase in Moragas' work characterized by an intense involvement in the field of industrial design and an in-depth study of residential typologies in which a synthesis of international models and local tradition serves as the basis for bringing together criteria of functionality, solidity and design of quality finishes.

The rational, expressive and always openly declared use of different materials for each system or construction element –concrete for the structure, brick for the skin of the facade, ceramic tiles for ornamental claddings, iron for the railings and other construction details, and wood for those elements more within the user's reach– results in a highly personal and easily identifiable architecture whose sincerity touches on brutalism. It is, moreover,

executed with a view to the practical needs of the users, who also benefit from the rationality of the layouts and the special attention paid by Moragas to the handling of the communal spaces – gardens, vestibules, stairs and distribution corridors serving the apartments. For these large multi-resident apartment buildings, Moragas habitually designed all of the detailing which contributes to the quality of the architecture (lighting, furniture, doorknockers, balustrades, etc.).

By the same architects and dating from the same period are the Cinema Liceo (c/ Sants, 96, 1957-1959), with its expressive facade reflecting the rational layout of the interior, and the apartment building at c/ Comte Borrell, 205-213 (1958).

Cinema Liceo.

Faculty of Law   1958

Av. de la Diagonal, 684
Guillermo Giráldez Dávila, Pedro López Inigo and
Xavier Subias Fages, architects
Bus 7, 75. Metro L3 (Palau Reial)

In December 1950, the Board of Works for the University Campus was officially constituted. In 1955, construction started on the first building, the Faculty of Pharmacology (initially intended to be a hall of residence), which was opened in 1957 and clearly bears the stamp of rhetorical academicism. Also from this period are two very ably executed buildings in exposed brickwork: the Sant Raimon de Penyafort and Nostra Senyora de Montserrat halls of residence (Av. de la Diagonal, 643, 1955-1958), designed by Pere Benavent de Barberà.

In order to remove the rebellious law students from the centre of the city, great urgency was attached to the brief for the new faculty building, which was drawn up in three months, and completed and opened only nine months later. This building, which manifests a surprising modernity of conception for an official commission of this period, testifies to the young Catalan architects' desire for innovation and for closer links with the Europran construction scene. It has been hailed by the critics as the prime example in Catalonia of the International Style. The rationality of the structure, giving a free floor plan allowing great functional diversity, is outstanding, as is the expressive handling of the materials used in the structure and the skin, the richness of the spaces, the interior courtyards, the relationship between exterior and interior and the carefully thought-out composition of the volumes, revealing the functional character of each one.

Halls of residence at Av. de la Diagonal, 643.

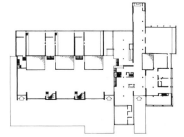

39
Mutua Metalúrgica de Seguros building

1955-1959

Av. de la Diagonal, 394-398; c/ Provença, 344
Oriol Bohigas Guardiola, Josep Martorell Codina, architects
Bus 6, 15, 33, 34, 43, 54. Metro L4, L5 (Verdaguer)

The volume as a whole is adapted to a trapezoidal plot typical of the passage of the Av. de la Diagonal through the regular Ensanche grid, with the narrowest facade marked by a slight buttress-like inflexion. The complexity of the programme (dispensaries, offices, surgical hospital, laboratories, convent, functions hall) called for a structure offering the maximum possible flexibility. This was duly resolved on the basis of a metal frame which declares its presence on the clad exterior. The envelope of the facades –which do not express the interior programme– combines the false curtain walls of the windows with the solid skin of pink granite in the interest of a more successful integration with the existing context. During 1967-1969 a swept-back attic volume with a copper roof was added to accommodate the convent.

The building features decorative ceramics and sculptures by Jordi Domènech, a photograph by Català Roca and paintings by F. Todó and R. Solanic. In the outdoor landscaped space which relates to the equivalent space on the ground floor, the sculpture "Ictineo" by Josep Maria Subirachs, dedicated to Narcís Monturiol, was unveiled on December 3rd, 1963.

Contemporary buildings by other architects include the Mandrí building (c/ Pau Claris, 180; c/ Provença, 277, from 1955-1959) by Josep Maria Fargas and Enric Tous; the office and apartment building (c/ Rosselló, 257, 1956-1963) by Robert Terradas Via, and the Clínica Sant Jordi (Via Augusta, 273, 1957) by Ricard Ribas Seva.

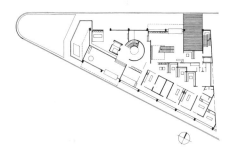

The building at c/ Rosselló, 257.

40
SEAT complex

1954-1960

Plaza Ildefons Cerdà. Zona Franca
Manuel Barbero, Rafael Echaíde Itarte, Rafael de la Joya,
César Ortiz Echagüe, architects

Alongside a traffic intersection dignified as a square –and all the more ironically named after Ildefons Cerdà, mastermind of the city's Ensanche grid– in the Zona Franca industrial estate, this complex of facilities was built by the state-owned SEAT car company in the mid-fifties.

This complex comprises: staff Canteen (Sector A, Street 2, 1-25; 1954-1956, by C. Ortiz, M. Barbero, R. de la Joya and R. Echaíde); the Laboratories (in the same sector; 1959-1960, by C. Ortiz and R. Echaíde); the Apprentices' School (Paseo de la Zona Franca, c/ Cisell; 1956-1957, by M. Barbero and R. de la Joya), a 54-metre tower (closest to the square) and a depot for cars (Plaza Ildefons Cerdà; Gran Via de les Corts Catalanes, 140; C. Ortiz, R. Echaíde), which received most acclaim from the architecture critics.

This cuboid with its six open-plan floors, backed by an annexe building containing the vehicle access ramp, has a continuous exposed portal frame structure (with a span of six metres, and twelve between pillars) painted matt black. The outer skin enveloping all of the facades is of aluminium and glass, allowing daylight into the building and producing diaphanous interior spaces that are perfectly visible from the exterior by day and night.

In the 1990s these buildings were massively altered (to the point of being unrecognisable) for conversion into apartments. Visiting them now is of no interest.

41
Apartment building

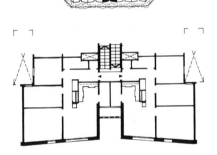 **1958-1959**

C/ Pallars, 299-317

Oriol Bohigas Guardiola, Josep Martorell Codina, architects

Bus 6, 40, 42, 141. Metro L4 (Poblenou)

The programme called for 130 apartments for metalworkers and their families, to be fitted into a volume that was to occupy one side of a typical Cerdà Ensanche block in a fairly peripheral part of the city.

The architects' response is a model solution in every respect. The block was subdivided into six bays, with four apartments to a floor, served by recessed communications cores, thus endowing the sober exposed brickwork facades with greater individuality, further reinforced by the zigzagging outline and the pointed silhouette. On reaching the chamfered corners at the ends of the city block, however, the external facades become flat planes, adroitly resuming the original alignment. Another inspired decision is the highly rational distribution of these modest apartments, comprising three bedrooms and a living-cum-dining room with kitchen within 60 m². All in all, and taking into account the use of traditional building systems and materials in an evidently sceptical repudiation of the ostenta-tiously innovative technologies then being essayed by the construction industry, this complex is a wholly authentic manifesto of the "realist" approach.

The same architects, with the addition of the architect David Mackay to the team, designed the apartment buildings at c/ Roger de Flor, 215 (1957-1958), at paseo de Maragall, 243-247 (1959) and at c/ Calvet, 71 (1960), all of which reinterpret organizational schemes and layouts first developed in the complex in c/ Escorial.

42
Apartment building   **1957-1961**

C/ Johann Sebastian Bach, 7-7 bis
José Antonio Coderch de Sentmenat and
Manuel Valls Vergès, architects
Bus 6, 7, 14, 33, 34, 66

This building was not well received by the wealthy bourgeoisie at whom it was aimed, on account of the simplicity of its materials and the sobriety of its formal premises. Coderch and Valls approached the design, once again, as an exercise in the reinterpretation of traditional architecture adapted to a modern programme, with the difficulty here that these were large apartments in a very exclusive residential neighbourhood.

The free-standing block is rectangular in plan, with its load-bearing walls parallel to the side facades, which are themselves structural, and its main facades conceived as large free openings filtered by the lightweight skin of wooden slats on the continuous terraces, with their triangular balconies, also partially enclosed; the continuous vertical sequence of these balconies produces volumes reminiscent of the traditional gallery.

The four apartments on each floor are ordered on the basis of two orthogonal axes disposed around a central well which ventilates the service rooms and the bedroom, developed in terms of a functional programme perfectly adapted to the envisaged type of occupant. The double circulation scheme serves the living and dining areas and the bedrooms and other rooms, laid out around a core composed of the hall and the lifts which provide direct access to each apartment.

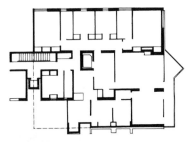

43
Casa de los Toros

1960-1962

Gran Via de les Corts Catalanes, 798-814
Antoni de Moragas Gallissà and
Francesc de Riba Salas, architects
Bus 6, 7, 18, 35, 56, 62

The experimental line in apartment buildings initiated by Moragas within the field of constructive realism in the building in c/ Sant Antoni M. Claret was continued and perfected in the Casa de los Toros. This complex is composed of three units, with eight apartments to a floor, occupying part of an Ensanche block, including the chamfered corner, making it necessary for one the general layout of one of the units to adapt to the form of the corner, while another benefits from the presence of the neighbouring church, towards which it opens another facade perpendicular to the Gran Via avenue.

The structure of reinforced concrete on the ground floors is crowned on the facade by large, expressive corbels which project out from the traditional load-bearing walls of the residential floors. The interior surfaces of the terraces and the communal vestibules were decorated with bullfighting photographs by Francesc Català Roca taken in the Monumental bullring, only a few metres from the building, much frequen-

ted by Moragas (and by other architects such as Coderch and Churruca).

Also by Moragas and Ribas from this period are the apartment buildings at c/ Padilla, 323-329 (1959-1963); at Av. Meridiana, 302-312 (1962), with an unusual and attractive treatment of the crowns of the facades; at Ronda de Sant Pau, 42-44 (1964); and at Via Augusta, 128-132, c/ Brusi, 39-45, c/ Sant Elies (1967-1970), and c/ Biscaia, 340 (1969-1970), in which the decorative solutions employed in the vestibules attain the greatest magnificence.

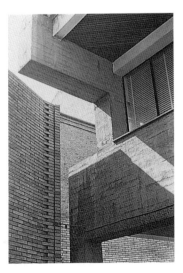

44
Sant Medir parish church   1958-1960
C/ de la Constitució, 17
Jordi Bonet Armengol, architect
Bus 91

The survival through to the fifties of an architecture immediately derived from Gaudí can be seen in Catalan religious buildings designed by architects who had had some direct or indirect contact with the great man. In his Sant Medir parish church, Jordi Bonet continues with the modern reworking of Gaudiesque themes undertaken by his father, Lluís Bonet Garí, architect of the Sant Miquel chapel in Argentona and the Passion facade of the Sagrada Família itself, begun in 1952 in collaboration with Isidre Puig Boada, who designed the Sagrat Cor church in Balaguer.

The complex programme for this parish church had to be resolved within a small gap site. Bonet introduced inwardly sloping perimeter walls for the nave, permitting him to roof the space without intermediate supports, using parabolic vaults whose exterior is partially treated with *trencadis* ceramic fragments. The priest's residence and various other parts of the programme had to be accommodated within the bell tower, a nine-storey cuboid which adopts a more conventional language.

The church of Sant Joan Maria Vianney (c/ Melcior de Palau, 60, 1952-1963), by Raúl Miguel Rivero, similarly pursues this Gaudiesque line. Also of interest from this period are the churches of Sant Ot (paseo Manuel Girona, 23-25, 1958-1960), by Francesco Salvans and Emilio Bordoy, with its references to contemporary European religious architecture, and Santa Tecla (Av. Madrid, 107, 1958), by J. Soteras, with a structure of concrete and iron. In 1961, the architect Sagnier Vidal completed the expiatory temple on the summit of Tibidabo, begun by his father in 1909.

45
School of Higher Business Studies 1954-1961
(Escuela Universitaria de Estudios Empresariales)
Av. de la Diagonal, 694
Javier Carvajal Ferrer and Rafael García de Castro, architects
F. Bassó Birulés (consultant architect)
Bus 7, 75. Metro L3 (Zona Universitària)

Designed four years earlier than the Faculty of Law, this building was not completed until several years later. The project –embodying a complex programme which required the differentiation of specific functions in independent and typologically distinct, yet organically interrelated volumes– explicitly echoes contemporary movements in international architecture in its application of a brutalist aesthetic.

The exposed structure is the dominant feature of the exterior elevations. On the great modular facade running parallel to the Diagonal, the voids are faced with lightweight materials prompted by a concern with taking maximum advantage of natural light –perhaps excessive, bearing in mind the insulation required by the building's orientation, surely evident from the outset, and the absence of elements to give protection from the sun– that is also apparent in the disposition of the rooflights and the cloistered spaces which determine the interior circulation scheme.

The year after the official opening of the School of Higher Business Studies saw the inauguration of the School of Architecture (the Escola Tècnica Superior d'Arquitectura, Diagonal, 649, 1961-1962) by Eusebi Bona, Pelayo Martínez and Josep M. Segarra, followed a little later by the School of Industrial Engineering, designed by Robert Terradas Via in 1959, once again with its classrooms set perpendicular to the Av. Diagonal.

Editorial Gustavo Gili

1954-1961

C/ Rosselló, 87-89

Francesc Bassó Birulés, Joaquim Gili Moros, architects

Bus 41. Metro L5 (Entença)

Situated in the interior of an Ensanche city block, with access from the street passing through a spacious landscaped courtyard, the complex is developed as three volumes, organically interrelated, yet each with an entirely different exterior resolution; this is apparent not only in the individualized definition of the volumes but in the formal discontinuity of the facades. In addition to the underground level occupied by the warehouses and general services, the building is laid out over two floors, with the exception of the entrance vestibule of the central volume, characterized by a double-height space with a mezzanine balcony. This mezzanine, with its sinuous perimeter, accommodates the circulation routes serving offices and meeting rooms.

The central volume, comprising the public area and the sales and technical departments, is the most interesting part of the complex, as much for the structural pillars supporting five triangular beams to form an outwardly projecting roof with a convex angular surface, as for the formal treatment of the main facade, on which the sunshades allow the creation of transparent spaces and an uninterrupted correlation between exterior and interior. Despite the requirements of its industrial and commercial programme, the complex has skilfully avoided the conventional typological resources generally encountered in buildings of this kind.

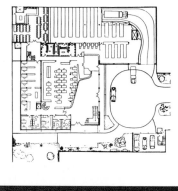

47
Manzana Seida   1955-1967

Av. de Sarrià, 130-152; ronda del General Mitre
Francesc Mitjans Miró, architect (petrol station and apartments), and
Josep Soteras Mauri, architect (garage and car-repair workshop)
Rafael Casals, engineer (petrol station)
Bus 6, 16, 33, 34, 66, 70, 74. FF.CC. Generalitat (Tres Torres)

The complex consists of a petrol station, which was constructed first (1955), a garage and car-repair workshop, and a block of apartments. The petrol station has a trapezoidal plan, and is characterized by its parabolic roof slab of reinforced concrete, with a maximum thickness of 7 cm, smooth on its underside and ribbed on the upper surface. This is supported by two great parabolic arches, rectangular in section, set 35 metres apart at ground level –closing to a span of 25 metres at roof level– which project up through the roof. These arches are provided with strut tenons to lessen the lateral projection of the roof slab.

In the residential block there is a marked contrast between the differing treatments of the facades on the basis of their orientation and position within the urban context. The Avinguda de Sarrià facade displays large expanses of glass and onderly terraces, emphatically horizontal, while the rear facade is organized as a series of individualized vertical volumes disposed in a denticu-lated arrangement, with blind side walls of exposed brickwork and concrete. The structural resolution of the garage is attractively handled.

Mitjans produced a number of other interesting residential buildings in this period: at c/ de Sant Adrià, 138-150 (1959-1962); the CYT building, at Via Augusta, 20-30 (1959-1960); at c/ Mestre Nicolau, 13 (1957-1960); at c/ Vallmajor, 18-20 (1955-1959), and the Tokio building, at Av. de Pedralbes, 59-61 (1957).

CYT building, Via Augusta, 20-30.

Apartment building

1959-1964

Ronda del General Mitre, 1-13 and 19-25
Francisco-Juan Barba Corsini, architect
Bus 6, 16, 66, 70, 74. FF.CC. Generalitat (Tres Torres)

Two circumstances conditioned the solution adopted by Barba Corsini –who designed a number of residential buildings of great quality in this period– for this block of shops and apartments: the form of the plot, which suggested dividing the building into two independent blocks, and the fact that this was a subsidized housing development ("controlled rent"), which imposed a maximum upward limit on the floor area of these apartments.

The building is composed of two parallel blocks, united by the vertical communications nuclei, with 15 apartments on each of the ten upper floors, rationally organized in pairs to allow concentration of services. The structure is of reinforced concrete and the exterior detailing in metal.

The facades are resolved on the basis of toughened glass curtain walls, shaded from the sun by the projecting terraces, with opaque screens for privacy. Barba Corsini adopted this same solution in his apartment building at c/ Escoles Pies, 20-22 (1960).

From 1954 to 1955, Barba Corsini carried out an extremely interesting conversion scheme in the attic space of the Casa Milà, "La Pedrera" (Paseo de Gràcia, 92) by Antoni Gaudí, creating a group of small flats, including a duplex apartment, for which he also designed the furniture.

Attic of La Pedrera.

49
Apartment building   1960-1962

C/ Johann Sebastian Bach, 28
Taller de Arquitectura (Ricardo Bofill Levi)
Bus 7, 14

This was one of the Taller de Arquitectura's first built schemes, directed by Ricardo Bofill, son of the local architect and developer Emili Bofill Benessat. The characteristics of the site (a rectangle with one facade looking north-west and 90% of the rest of the perimeter bounded by existing buildings) determined the adoption of an unconventional approach to the positioning and distribution of the two apartments per floor. Following a north-south axis, the vertical circulation core is succeeded by an interior courtyard, which receives direct sunlight and opens onto the large courtyard in the centre of the block. The four bedrooms, arranged in a zig-zag sequence, look onto this interior patio, from which they receive natural light and ventilation. The living areas of the two apartments are organized

asymmetrically in the bay of the facade, with the services inserted into the remaining space of the complex plan.

The building has a mixed structure, with load-bearing walls and pillars, and the outer skin of the main facade is finished with ceramic blinds over the dining area and sliding lattice blinds in front of the living area. Between these, and effectively separating them, is the projecting volume of the terrace. The use of these materials on the facade skilfully resolves the problem of controlling daylight and the relationship between interior and exterior.

The apartment building at number 2 of the same street, on the corner of the plaza de Sant Gregori Taumaturg, was designed and constructed by the Taller during 1962 and 1963.

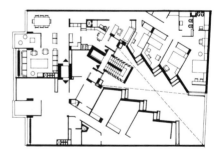

Colegio de Arquitectos de Cataluña y Baleares   **1958-1962**

Plaza Nova, 5

Xavier Busquets Sindreu, architect

Bus 16, 17, 19, 45. Metro L1, L2, L3 (Catalunya), L4 (Jaume I)

Given the situation of the site, in the vicinity of major architectonic landmarks of the historic city, the project (winner of the competition organized by the architects' professional association) declared a clear intention of breaking away from conventional ideas of the integration of new building into the historic fabric, a question which then constituted one of the key debates in architecture.

The building consists of a low, forward-projecting volume with a trapezoidal plan, entirely glazed on the ground floor and blind above, which accommodates the public areas (bar, exhibition space, reception and functions hall), and an eight-storey office tower with the vertical circulation nucleus and services backing onto it. The metal bearing structure of the tower is exposed, as is the system supporting the curtain wall, the vertical distribution and proportion of which was altered by Alfons Milà in 1971 with the addition of fibre-reinforced concrete panels on top of the original skin, and square window-blinds.

The sgraffito designed by Picasso (and drawn in situ by Carl Nesjar) for the exterior walls of the low building and the vestibule of the functions hall have now become a part of the itinerary of tourists visiting the old city. Another point of interest here is the fact that different architects were invited to design the interiors of the upper floors (Moragas; Correa-Milà; Fargas-Tous; Bohigas-Martorell-Mackay; Monguió-Vayreda; Giráldez-López Iñigo-Subias; Bassó-Gili). However, these original design schemes have since been overtaken by the continual and not always felicitous remodelling of the interiors.

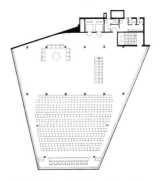

Original plan of the functions hall.

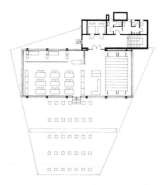

Original distribution of the second floor.

51
Montbau housing estate   **1957-1965**

Paseo de la Vall d'Hebron; c/ Arquitectura; c/ Poesia
Guillermo Giráldez, Pedro López Íñigo and Xavier Subias,
architects (Partial Plan and sector 1); Manuel Baldrich,
Antoni Bonet and Josep Soteras, architects (sector 2)
Bus 27, 73, 76, 85. Metro L3 (Montbau)

The 1953 General Urban Plan for Barcelona envisaged the construction of a major hospital complex in this area, and a residential development which was developed in the subsequent Partial Plan. The basic ideas of the urban design scheme were the following: to create a unitary nucleus of dwellings with a character of their own, on the basis of free-standing blocks; to organize and differentiate the civic and commercial zones as elements of spatial articulation; to create landscaped spaces as centres for play and recreation; to utilize the public buildings as focal points in the composition, and to clearly distinguish pedestrian and vehicle circulation routes.

The complex as a whole was ordered in three super-blocks: one to the north-east, with the better quality housing in blocks of different heights with a landscaped space in the interior; another to the west, with the volumes laid out geometrically around a central courtyard, while the third is the commercial area, composed of individual buildings forming semi-enclosed spaces.

Critics today tend to regard this complex as the best example of the application of the CIAM's methods and criteria to the realities of urban design in Barcelona. Other contemporary housing estates include Sant Martí (c/ Bac de Roda, Gran Via, c/ Guipúscoa, 1956-1958); the one to the south-west of the Besòs river (c/ Llull, c/ Prim and Gran Via, 1958-1966), and the Milans del Bosch group of apartment buildings (c/ Sant Adrià, 196, 1962-1964), this last by Bohigas, Martorell and Mackay.

52
Former Joyería Monés   1959-1962

C/ Guillem Tell, 47; c/ Lincoln, 36-38
Joan Antoni Ballesteros Figueras, Joan Carles Cardenal
González, Francesc de la Guàrdia Conte, Pere Llimona Torras and
Xavier Ruiz Vallès, architects
Bus 16, 17, 27, 30. FF.CC. Generalitat (Plaça Molina)

The building, originally designed for use as offices and a jewelry factory, is laid out over seven floors (including basement and semi-basement). The four upper floors compose a perfect cuboid, solid in appearance, of plane surfaces clad in pearl grey stoneware tiling, in contrast to the lower floors with their exposed structure and lightweight envelope, the ground floor being contained within a continuous free-standing wall clad in dark green granite.

On the side facades of the upper volume, the plane surface is only broken by a single, full-height vertical slit next to the rear arris. On the main facade, the great glazed expanse of the first three floors is protected by a continuous system of movable blinds. The flat roof is concealed behind the opaque crown, with its single rectangular opening invoking the language of rationalism.

The structure is of pillars and flat beams of reinforced concrete and ceramic floor slabs, and the walls are of cellular brick.

Another interesting industrial building from this period is the Laboratorios Ubach (c/ Degà Bahí, 67, 1958-1961), noteworthy for the plane facade of the main volume and the glazed stair well on the interior facade. The same architect, Manuel Ribas Piera, also designed the parish dispensary of Nostra Senyora del Port (1958).

Facade of the Laboratorios Ubach building.

53
House and studio for Antoni Tàpies 1960-1963

C/ Saragossa, 57

José Antonio Coderch de Sentmenat and Manuel Valls Vergès, architects

Bus 16, 17, 27, 30. FF.CC. Generalitat (Plaça Molina, Sant Gervasi)

This house for the Catalan painter Antoni Tàpies has long been considered a masterpiece of private domestic urban architecture. Constructed on a deep, narrow (eight metres) gap site, and opening only onto one noisy street in the Sant Gervasi district, the multiple functional programme (apartments for the painter and the caretakers, workshop and studio) is laid out over five floors that step back in the interior to overlook the courtyard in the centre of the block.

The facade overlooking the street, from which the interior is insulated as far as possible, is resolved in terms of an envelope of fibre-reinforced cement panels, ordered into six modules divided by the exposed concrete structure, painted white, and differently proportioned in each module in relation to the use of space determined by the interior programme.

The supreme accomplishment of the building is found in the distribution and illumination of the interior spaces. The entire building is organized as a succession of open and closed spaces set around the interior courtyard, with the stairs climbing around it, in which the oblique sightlines terminate with the varnished brickwork of the walls. At

the rear of the plot, on the ground floor, is the painter's double-height studio. The main apartment is situated under the library, which insulates itself by turning its inset blind back wall on the street, and opens onto the courtyard in the interior of the block.

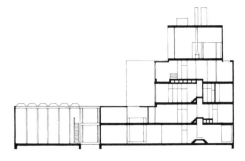

Canódromo Meridiana

1962-1963

C/ Concepción Arenal, 165

Antoni Bonet Castellana and Josep Puig Torné, architects

Bus, 11, 12, 34, 62. Metro L1 (Fabra i Puig)

The dog track is situated in a rectangular block, and consists of a building laid out along one of the longer sides, and the elongated ellipse of the track, with its semi-circular ends. The built volume is defined by two floors in the form of concentric parabolas with a difference of 2 metres in their foci. The bearing structure of steel pillars and the sunscreen which rises up over the stand are the most expressive elements in the construction.

The floor slab on the first floor is of reinforced concrete and concrete caissons, while the stand uses beams in tension and industrial concrete elements. The roof beams transmit their load to a central pillar, with a projection of 10 metres, supported at its furthest point by a vertical triangular element, directed down onto the lower level, which takes the weight of the sunshade. On the rear facade, vertical tensors join the structure to the lower roof to prevent movement; the main roof beams are stabilized by triangular transverse lattice straps on which the insulation rests.

These two architects also produced the Mediterráneo building, at c/ Consell de Cent, 162-180 (1960-1966), which boasts a remarkable reinforced concrete structure. The Torre Urquinaona, at Plaza Urquinaona, 6 and c/ Roger de Llúria, 1-3 (1970-1973), and the Torre Cervantes, in c/ Manuel Ballbé, 3-5, are by Antoni Bonet and Benito Miró Llort.

The Torre Urquinaona.

55
Hispano Olivetti office building   1960-1964

Ronda de la Universitat, 18
Ludovico Belgiojoso, Enrico Peressutti and Ernesto N. Rogers, architects
Collaborators: J. Soteras (site supervision) and R. Casals (engineer)
Bus 14, 16, 17, 24, 55, 58, 59, 66. Metro L1, L3 (Catalunya), L2 (Universitat)
FF.CC. Generalitat (Catalunya)

Since the 19th century, the question of how to intervene in a historic setting has troubled architectural thinking. The Modern Movement effectively exploded the issue, but it reappeared in Italy after the war. The polemic concerning the siting of the new Col.legi d'Arquitectes building in the historic heart of the city was Barcelona's first taste of the dispute. In the Ensanche, on the other hand, the existing buildings had never conditioned the new architecture. The character of the setting ought to be taken into account, but it should not be allowed to define the stylistic aspects of the new construction. This principle was clearly accepted by everyone from the masters of Modernisme through to the rationalists.

From the fifties on, all of this changed. The "existing environmental features" of an already amply historical Ensanche had to be respected: the new, cultured architecture would have to "integrate". The matter of how this was to be done gave rise to an interesting and still unresolved debate. With the rejection of pastiche –which did not reappear in Barcelona until a by-law set out to "save" the Ensanche– one possible option was the reinterpretation of the essential features of the urban context.

This was the path chosen by the BPR group here, in this office building whose open-plan floors are enclosed by a curtain-wall that is stepped in plan, seen by the critics as a –by all means free– interpretation of one existing feature of the setting: the typical glazed gallery of the *Modernista* Ensanche house.

Apartment building   1959-1966

Av. de la Meridiana, 312 bis-318

Oriol Bohigas, Josep Martorell and David Mackay, architects

Bus 62. Metro L1, L5 (Sagrera)

The basic conception of this group of 121 minimal apartments (less than 60 m²) for a housing cooperative is a direct consequence of the economic and urbanistic conditions and the orientation of the plot. On top of a freer lower floor, with an exposed concrete structure on the facade, stand eleven floors of apartments. The structure of load-bearing walls constitutes the two groups of residential modules aligned with each of the facades –with their ceramic cladding and loops and projections of exposed concrete– between which the vertical communications nuclei separate five sizeable interior wells.

The openings in the facade, which turn away from the northward orientation in the interests of visual privacy and acoustic insulation, have been gi-ven a highly unusual treatment. Conceived as projecting angular double galleries, these adopt a variety of dispositions "according to a complex pre-established geometrical rhythm" as a means of endowing each apartment with a distinct personality and breaking the monotony which seems so inescapable in this type of building. The heterogeneous transformations which these openings have undergone in the course of thirty years are the occupants' own, perhaps unintentional, contributions to the architects' concern with individualization, as well as being a legitimate response to the shortcomings of the original construction. There seem, then, to be no grounds for lamenting the alterations that the building has experienced since it was first occupied.

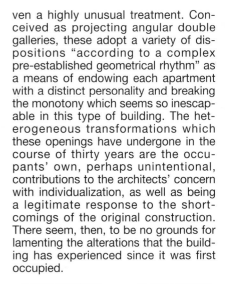

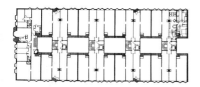

57
Apartment building
(Casa del Pati)   **1961-1964**

Ronda del Guinardó, 42-44; c/ Lepant, (unnumbered)
Oriol Bohigas, Josep Martorell and David Mackay, architects
Bus 25, 401. Metro L4 (Alfons X)

The residential architecture of MBM, without ever abandoning the pursuit of the greatest rationality in the interior distribution of the apartments and in the relationship between economic factors and construction system (the basis of "realism"), has increasingly stressed the importance of the ordering of the whole so as to give the communal spaces the leading role they deserve. This concern takes on the character of a manifesto in this building, with its apartments grouped around a spacious well which in addition to its function of ventilation assumes the role of social and circulation space, offering sanctuary from the aggressive exterior environment. The spatial and formal treatment of this courtyard evokes an urban public space, with the fountain in the vestibule contributing to the poetics of the overall conception.

The same concern for the communal spaces can be seen in the Xaudiera house (c/ Entença, 99-101, 1964-1970), today in a woeful state of disrepair out of all proportion to its age. Also by the MBM team are the apartment buildings at Ronda del Guinardó, 46 (1961-1964) and 54-56 (1967-1969).

With regard to the integration of new architecture into a historic context, a central issue in the architectural thinking of the time, the MBM team made an intelligent contribution to the debate with their La Vanguardia apartment and print-workshop building (c/ Tallers, 52-54, 1962-1965).

58
El Redemptor church

Av. de la Mare de Déu de
Montserrat, 34-40

1957-1963
1962-1968 (construction)

Oriol Bohigas, Josep Martorell and David Mackay, architects

Bus 31, 32, 39, 55

The site, in the interior of a closed residential block not originally designed to accommodate a building of this kind, suggested maintaining the street alignment by means of the wall of the courtyard-entrance atrium and the setting back of the volume of the nave. This was clearly intended to promote the integration of the building into its surroundings without detracting from its character as an outstanding element –in terms of function and volumetry– in the urban fabric.

The nave is trapezoidal in plan, with the shortest side, the exposed brick end wall, folded inward in the middle, receiving natural light by way of two openings situated at the intersection with the longer side walls –also of exposed brickwork– and giving a focal character to the chancel, which is devoid of any other element of significance. The relationship between the chancel (with its free-standing altar) and the body of the church (with four files of pews facing the altar) is entirely traditional.

The structure of the roof is of articulated wooden trusses supported on free-standing wooden posts, with the non-structural nature of the walls being emphasized by the continuous horizontal band of glazing which lets daylight into the nave.

The same architects also designed the churches of Sant Sebastià del Verdum (Via Favència; 1958) and Sant Josep Obrer (c/ Palamós, 35), as well as the Sant Sebastià Parochial Centre (c/ Viladrosa, 96; 1960-1968). In this last scheme, the disposition of the church in plan is closer to the liturgical recommendations of the Second Vatican Council.

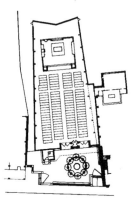

59
Apartment building

1962-1964

C/ Nicaragua, 97-99; c/ Marquès de Setmenat, 68
Taller de Arquitectura (Ricardo Bofill Levi)

Bus 15, 43, 54, 59

The programme was a difficult one: three flats to a floor on a small, badly oriented triangular gap site. The handling of the plan, and thus of the facade, was thought out on the basis of these conditioning factors, as the Taller had earlier done with the building at c/ Johann Sebastian Bach, 28.

The axis of the plot situates the stairs and, opening onto the facade, the main apartment. The other two flats open onto the facade and the sunny courtyard to the rear. In all three, almost half of the total area of 75 m² is given over to the living room. The facade has been conceived as a fan of walls –virtually blind on their north face– with the rooms opening to the exterior in the interstices, oriented to catch the sun. Starting from this idea, and with the fine exposed brickwork of the construction, the building achieves considerable expressive effects, particularly on the ground floor and the attics. In short, an example of good architecture created as a rational, creative and expressive response to a coherent appraisal of requirements and conditions.

The apartment building at c/ Viladomat, 297 (1965-1966), reveals the same concern with the rational distribution of a small surface area, although it is already possible to discern here the first symptoms of that neglect of the construction aspects in favour of purely formal considerations that becomes more pronounced in the Taller's subsequent work.

House at c/ Viladomat, 297.

Printroom and offices for
El Noticiero Universal   **1963-1965**

C/ Roger de Llúria, 35

Josep Maria Sostres Maluquer, architect

Bus 22, 24, 28, 39, 45, 47. Metro L3, L4 (Passeig de Gràcia)

As in the case of the Olivetti offices, the architectural critics considered the Noticiero building as an example of the successful integration of new architecture into the Barcelona Ensanche. On this occasion, however, the process was very different. Josep Maria Sostres, a founder member and the first theorist of Grup R, was thoroughly imbued with the teachings of the Modern Movement, and it was not to be expected that in his first engagement with the Ensanche –for all his awareness that "integration" was inevitable– he would opt for the revisionist postures then in vogue.

In his design for El Noticiero, Sostres made no attempt to reinterpret any of the existing qualities of the Ensanche (neither typological, nor constructive, and still less stylistic) or to establish formal correspondences; he engages in dialogue with the existing context, but in terms of the most absolute autonomy, ensuring that his architecture keeps faith with itself. The facade of the new building, with its free floor plan, expresses its non-structural character in the horizontality of its openings. The smooth plane of the facade, with no cornice, is further evidence of the most orthodox rationalism. The only concessions to the context are the use of stone in the curtain-wall and the subdivision into vertical elements of the conceptual horizontal opening. A dialogue that is perhaps excessively subtle.

In the Ciutat Diagonal residential development in the neighbouring town of Esplugues de Llobregat, Sostres built two of his most significant works, the Iranzo house (1957) and the MMI house (1957-1958).

61
Faculty of Economic Science   **1964-1967**

Av. de la Diagonal, 690
Guillermo Giráldez Dávila, Pedro López Íñigo and
Xavier Subias Fages, architects
Bus 7, 75. Metro L3 (Palau Reial, Zona Universitària)

The various rooms are grouped around the circulation scheme, and articulated by means of interior courtyards, following a complicated modular sequence. The classrooms, laid out in a comb-like formation, are ventilated by landscaped courtyards with no exterior views. The generally horizontal composition is broken only by the cylinder of the assembly hall and the taller volume of the seminar building.

The structure is mixed, with the vertical members of steel and the horizontal members of concrete. The expressive impact of the composition derives from the "brutalist" exposure of these members, in particular the potent double girders, and from the white concrete blinds of the assembly hall and the seminar building. The skin enclosing the north and south elevations of the latter volume is of panels of acid-washed concrete. The other opaque facades are of brick, either exposed (in interior as well as exterior spaces, facilitating their integration) or clad with dark brown stoneware tiling.

A total area of 15,250 m² was constructed for a maximum capacity of 1,968 students, equivalent to 7.74 m² per student. Between 1990 and 1993, the faculty building was extended to the east by the original architects, maintaining the original compositional and construction criteria.

Other university buildings of note from this same decade are those for the faculties of Philosophy and Geography and History (c/ Baldiri Reixac, unnumbered; 1969), by José Mª García-Valdecasas Salgado and Robert Terradas Via, where the programme is developed in separate blocks linked by glazed corridors.

Madre Güell students' hall of residence

1963-1967

C/ Esperança, 5-7
Lluís Cantallops Valeri and Jaume Rodrigo Dalmau, architects
Bus 22, 64, 75. FF.CC Generalitat (Sarrià)

The legacy of the realist premisses advanced by Bohigas and Martorell in the fifties declares itself in this architecture, fully identifying as it does with the formal approach that has come to be known as the "Barcelona school", and practised here by members of a younger generation of architects whose work finds in the Madre Güell students' residence one of its paradigms.

The project openly acknowledges the use of traditional materials and construction techniques, with the aim of expressing in terms of this language the pleasure to be derived from vernacular architecture and the relativity of advanced technology. The structure of load-bearing walls, the ceramic floor slabs, the Catalan vaulted ceilings, and the exposed brickwork facades (with their finely laid string courses and soldier courses on the window ledges) exhibit this combined constructive and symbolic value.

The H-shaped plan of the residence –a free-standing five-storey block neatly exploiting the dimensions of the plot– provides two independent courtyards for the use of the nuns and the female students.

Contemporary with the Madre Güell residence, and inviting comparison with it, is the Hotel Antibes (c/ Diputació, 394, c/ Sicilia; 1963-1964), by the architects Jacint Cánoves Richart and Manuel Francés Marqueta. Here the realist statement made by the exposed brickwork is set in the context of a smoothly expressive facade far removed from any kind of decorative rhetoric.

63
Apartment building

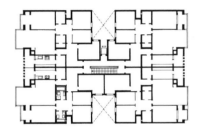

1966-1967

C/ Lepant, 307
Vicenç Bonet Ferrer, Lluís Nadal Oller and
Pere Puigdefàbregas Baserba, architects
Bus 9, 38, 72

The plan is symmetrically oriented on the basis of two orthogonal axes –which accommodate the single-flight stair and the lift– with four apartments to a floor. The interior distribution (four bedrooms, living-cum-dining room and services) reflects a rational scheme derived from the construction system of load-bearing walls. The kitchen opens onto the facade to keep the interior courtyards, reserved for the bedrooms, free of cooking smells. The services ventilate onto lightwells.

The existing built environment of the Sagrada Familia neighbourhood in which the building stands seem to invite the *Modernista* connotations so much in fashion at this time. The careful treatment of the exposed brickwork, the partial enclosing of the gallery-like terraces, the cladding of glazed ceramic tiles in the vestibule and the inner faces of the terraces, etc., invoke this context at the same time as they vindicate the vernacular.

The same architects also designed the La Vinya group of apartments (c/ Alts Forns-c/ Ferrocarrils Catalans; 1966-1968), where the traditional construction systems and materials and the austerity of the language are in keeping with the limited budget.

In the apartment building at c/ Rosselló, 152 (1964-1966) by J. Emili Donato Folch, the vindication of tradition and rationalism has resolved the street facade in a manner characteristic of the interior elevation typical of the Barcelona Ensanche.

Apartment building at c/ Rosselló, 152.

Apartment building

1964-1967

C/ Muntaner, 271; c/ Avenir, 35-37
Manuel de Solà-Morales Rosselló and
Manuel de Solà-Morales Rubió, architects
Bus 14, 58, 64. FF.CC. Generalitat (Muntaner)

The northward orientation of the corner formed by the two exterior elevations was once again here a decisive factor in the design of the plan –with six apartments to a floor, and one flight of stairs between two apartments– and thus also of the facades of this building, resolved with expressive sobriety.

All of the openings on the street facades, including the galleries stacked close to the corner, correspond to bedrooms. Those openings which do not project out are grouped, in pairs or singly, in vertical columns flanked by header bricks interrupted by the impost lines, inset in places and obtruding in others, that order the exposed brickwork of the facades, in which solid predominates over void. The presence of the three flights of stairs is marked on the facades by three projecting vertical volumes: five-sided, with a central opening, these are set between the sequences of windows.

Three pairs of corridors communicate this compact L-shaped exterior volume, occupied by the bedrooms, with a second built volume in the interior, opening onto the courtyard in the middle of the block. This contains the kitchens and living and dining areas, flanked by south-facing terraces. This volume, with an extra floor of attics, is separated from the bedrooms by four light wells, irregular in plan and larger in area than required by building regulations.

65
Calatrava apartment building   **1964-1968**

C/ Calatrava, 2-6; Via Augusta; c/ Rosari
Pere Llimona Torras and Xavier Ruiz Vallès, architects
Bus 14, 16, 70, 74. FF.CC. Generalitat (Tres Torres)

This building has been regarded as deriving from the postulates of Mies van der Rohe, no doubt on account of the rigorous calligraphy of its facades, executed in traditional materials: the exposed brickwork of the skin and the iron structural members –worked with great care– that reveal themselves on the exterior and order the composition.

The building is composed of two rectangular-based cuboids (with their longer axes at right angles), each containing six apartments, set one above another, with a floor area of 300 m^2 each. The vertical communications core is located between these two volumes. The subdivision into two blocks, and the relative position of these, provided for a better distribution of the apartments, with all of the rooms opening to the exterior and communicating by means of a circulation route running around the vestibule and the lift which opens directly into it.

The same architects put forward a similar proposal, apart from the obvious differences in situation and plot, in their apartment building at Via Augusta, 242 (1964-1968), the winner of the FAD Architecture Award for 1968 in the year that the jury fiercely debated the relative merits of the Banca Catalana headquarters by Tous and Fargas, and the Trade buildings by Coderch.

The building at Via Augusta, 242.

Banca Catalana

1965-1968

Paseo de Gràcia, 84

Josep Maria Fargas Falp and Enric Tous Carbó, architects

Bus 2, 22, 28. Metro L3 (Diagonal)

Fargas and Tous, determined to bring to bear the advantages of technology in spite of the conceptual hostility of the local architectural orthodoxy of the time, and the inertia of the construction industry, managed to produce works of great formal interest. The most successful of these is their head office for the Banca Catalana. Its facade is still, almost thirty years later, considered to be one of the most beautiful to be created in the Barcelona Ensanche since Modernisme, some outstanding examples of which are its immediate neighbours (the bank building is barely fifty metres from Gaudí's Casa Milà).

The Banca Catalana is resolved on the basis of a modular alternation of sheets of reflective thermal glass and parabolically curved industrial insulation panels –which the architects had already used on other occasions– in a system designed to allow for easy modification of the two elements when the interior function so required. The lower line of panels conceals the great structural support for the upper part of the building, enabling the complete trans-

parency of the ground floor, attracting the client and the passing pedestrian and facilitating the entry and exit of vehicles.

In the same line of experimentation, Fargas and Tous designed two further buildings for Banca Catalana, one at c/ Balmes, 236-238 (1975), now occupied by a ministry of the autonomous government, and the other at av. Diagonal, 662 (1974-1975). In the latter, the vegetation has been left to overgrow the facades in order to create its own exterior landscape.

The former Banca Catalana building in c/ Balmes.

67
Trade buildings

1966-1968

Gran Via de Carles III, 86-94

José Antonio Coderch de Sentmenat and Manuel Valls Vergès, architects

Bus 6, 7, 16, 34, 59, 66, 70, 72, 75. Metro L3 (Maria Cristina)

Coderch reinterpreted, in this group of four blocks for offices, some of the themes and experiences of the masters of the Modern Movement, both in his use of the curtain-wall as a uniform skin, and in the capacity of the volumes to constitute their own unique element of urban reference, a strategy particularly justified in sites –such as this zone between the Diagonal and the new ring road then was– without a defined urban morphology.

The curvilinear plan –decidedly at variance with the uncompromising angularity of those Modern masters' buildings– endows the four buildings with a deliberate uniqueness, emphasized by the beauty of the solution with which the curve is adopted by the metalwork elements of the curtain-wall, which thus resembles a real curtain in rippling motion.

In 1974, Coderch had a hand in defining the volumetry and skin of the Caixa de Pensions buildings (Av. Diagonal, 621), which make clear reference to the neighbouring Trade buildings. During the sixties, the use of the curtain-wall became widespread in Barcelona, especially in office buildings, but more as a symbolic statement of modernity than from any conviction of a constructive or urbanistic nature. One of the few noteworthy examples not already mentioned here is the Catalana de Occidente building (Av. Diagonal, 652-656; 1979) by the architect Pere Tomàs de Villota Rocha, which also makes telling use of curving forms.

Torre Colón Building
1965-1971

C/ Portal de Santa Madrona, 10-12; av. Drassanes, 6-8
Josep Anglada Rosselló, Daniel Gelabert Fontova and
Josep Ribas González, architects
Bus 14, 18, 36, 57, 64, 91. Metro L3 (Drassanes)

The construction of outstandingly tall buildings, although already a feature of Barcelona in the fifties, became in the course of the sixties the visible symbol of the high real-estate values which contemporary legislation then specifically fostered.

The Colón skyscraper, standing only a few metres from the mediaeval shipyards, is a paradigm of this class of buildings. The warping of the facades, with their decorated concrete parapets, and the striking hexagonal volume of the crown, topped by the great projecting inverted pyramid, make the tower a unique architectonic object which has become a landmark in the topography of the city.

Other buildings within this same category are the Autopistas building (Travessera de Gràcia, 101; 1963-1967) by Claudio Carmona; the Casa de los Médicos (plaza de Tetuan, 40; 1967-1972) by Marino Canosa and J. A. Comas de Mendoza; the new City Hall (plaza de Sant Miquel; 1962-1968) by Lorenzo García-Barbón, and the Banco de Comercio (plaza de Francesc Macià, 7; 1966-1973) by J. Soteras. Amongst the more accomplished examples are the Banco Atlántico (c/ Balmes, 168-170; 1966-1969) by Francesc Mitjans

and Santiago Balcells Gorina; the Banco de Sabadell (c/ Rosselló, 216; 1969-1972) by M. Francés Marqueta and B. Miró Llort, and the Patronato de Funcionarios Municipales block (c/ Wellington, 43; 1972) by J. Seguí, P. Monguió and F. Vayreda. The facades of various of these buildings are decorated with reliefs by Josep M. Subirachs, at that time the sculptor most in favour with public and financial institutions.

The Torre Colón.

The new city hall.

The Patronato de Funcionarios Municipales building.

69
Atalaya building

1966-1970

Av. de Sarrià, 71; av. de la Diagonal
Federico Correa Ruiz, Alfonso Milá Sagnier and
José Luis Sanz Magallón, architects
Bus 6, 7, 33, 34, 66

By the time Correa constructed his first building in Barcelona, he had already exerted a considerable influence on younger generations of architects through his teaching and a important body of work largely in the fields of interior design and private family houses.

The Atalaya building can be regarded as one of the few interesting contributions to the architecture of one-off towers that irrupted on the Barcelona of this period. The plan is composed of four volumes set in the form of a swastika with arms of unequal length, with the vertical communications core in the centre. The lowest floors serve as offices, with the remainder being residential, except for the top floor, which was to be occupied by a restaurant. The fa-cades, with their industrial construction elements in white artificial stone, reflect that variety of use, the higher group of floors projecting out more than the lower, with the top floor assuming a massively solid appearance.

The siting of the building, with its wider elevation perpendicular to the Diagonal, means that it is most frequently seen from an angle which manifests its least slender aspect.

The same studio went on a little later to design the Monitor building, at av. Diagonal, 670-672 (1968-1970), which reveals the evident influence of Coderch, in whose office both Federico Correa and Alfonso Milá had gained their early experience.

Atalaya. *Plan of floors 16 to 20.*

Atalaya. *Plan of floors 4 to 15.*

Atalaya.

Monitor building.

Clínica Corachán (extension)   1969

C/ de Buïgas, 19; plaza de Gironella, 4
Jaume Sanmartí Verdaguer, architect
Bus 16, 70, 74. FF.CC. Generalitat (Tres Torres)

This piece of work, approached with all the ambition of a young advocate of "total design", reveals the influence of contemporary Italian architecture –which underpins the so-called "Barcelona school"– that had captured the imaginations of the younger generation of Catalan architects of which Sanmartí was a member. The unbuilt project for the ESADE school by Federico Correa –the most important representative of this line of influence– can be discerned in this and in many other works by that generation of architects.

These influences, together with other indigenous factors, produced a series of architectures (some of enduring interest, such as the house at c/ Nàpols, 215, constructed by Jordi Llorens Perelló in 1970) whose less self-critical derivatives were to shape the Barcelona of the next decade (one example being the Blau building at plaça Lesseps, 33, by Albert Danés Tejedor, from 1970). The prime mover of this rhetorical dead-end may be considered as being the mannerist architecture of Miguel Alvarez Trincado,

responsible for the Cooperativa Sant Genís, at c/ Costa Pacheco, 27 (1968-1969).

Representing this same generation of architects, albeit in an individual and very different line, is the work of the architect Rafael Serra Florensa, and in particular his Club Deportivo Hispano-Francés in the Vall d'Hebron (Camí de Sant Cebrià; 1969).

House at c/ Nàpols, 215.

71
Casa Fullà

1967-1971

C/ Gènova, 27
Lluís Clotet Ballús and Òscar Tusquets Guillén, architects

Bus 31, 32, 39, 55

The late sixties brought signs of a change in Catalan architecture. In the approach to problems and solutions, correctness (that continuing legacy of the first phase of *Noucentisme*) was giving way to imagination. In terms of formal resolution, the perennial influence of the Italians was being replaced by, amongst other things, that of certain American architects. This spirit of innovation found in Oscar Tusquets and Lluís Clotet, at that time partners in the Studio PER, two of its leading exponents, and in the Casa Fullà, a significant landmark.

The variety of apartment types, the irregular form of the chamfered corner plot, the height of the neighbouring buildings, the concern with exploiting to the full the space available for construction and, above all, the desire to break with convention, all determined a solution that in its function as much as in the design of the facade is strikingly unusual.

The apartments are laid out over one, two or three levels, with the resulting spatial richness which no doubt serves to compensate the occupants (perhaps themselves as individual as their building) for the inevitable inconvenience this entails. The interior complexity is not exhibited on the facade, whose volumetry and construction elements (windows, balustrades, etc.) evidence a deliberate defiance of established norms.

A contemporary exercise by the same architects is their extension to an apartment building at c/ Sant Màrius, 36 (1969-1971), in which the choice of materials for the facade is itself an aspect of the imaginative design solution.

Section through the Casa Fullà.

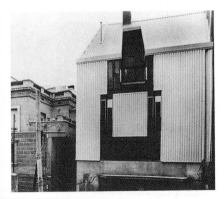

The house at c/ Sant Màrius, 36.

Casa Fullà.

72
Diagonal-Carles III underpass   **1971**

Av. de la Diagonal - Gran Via de Carles III
Carlos Fernández Casado, engineer
Bus 6, 7, 59, 70, 72, 75. Metro L3 (Maria Cristina)

Barcelona's urban transformation during the early seventies (in particular the opening of the Ronda del Mig and the upgrading of accesses to the city) produced a highly interesting series of engineering works by Carlos Fernández Casado which enriched the urban landscape of Barcelona in a field –public inrastructures– that had not before received the attention it deserved.

The most significant of these is this underpass running beneath the Diagonal (carried out in collaboration with the engineers Bernardo Monclús Jurado and Jaime Teulón), whose structural audacity (a length of 156 m and a span of 36 m without supports) and design quality won it a place in the finals of the FAD Architecture Awards.

Other works by Fernández Casado are: the plaza Ildefons Cerdà traffic distributor (1970-1971), with its three viaducts with a maximum span of 36 m; the plaza d'Espanya underpass (1970-1971), with reliefs by Subirachs; the pedestrian bridge over the Gran Via de Carles III at the carrer de Mejia Lequerica junction (1970-1973), with its three piers and projecting stair on the west access; the overpass, with a 24 m span, and the concrete footbridges in the plaza de les Glòries Catalanes (1973), demolished in the 1992 remodelling of the zone, and the metal footbridge suspended from tensed cables in the same zone (1972), with a free span of 96 m between the supports at either end (which won the Premio Nacional de Estructuras Metálicas award in 1975 and the European Convention of Metal Constructions prize), moved in 1992 to a site on the new Ronda del Litoral.

73
Raset complex of residential blocks

1967-1973

C/ Raset, 21-31; c/ Freixa, 22-32
José Antonio Coderch de Sentmenat and Manuel Valls Vergès, architects
Bus 14. FF.CC. Generalitat (La Bonanova)

The proprietors of the site, following the standard urban development practice of the time, had intended the plot –in a low-rise neighbourhood– for a tower block of considerable height. The architects proposed as an alternative a group of six smaller buildings, ordered symmetrically in two sets of three, with communal spaces related to the landscaped setting and the surrounding streets. The height of the resulting blocks and the stepped form of the higher volumes facilitate integration into the context.

On each floor there are two large apartments, divided into three distinct zones, whose distribution in plan recalls Coderch and Valls' famous single-family houses: bedrooms aligned and set back, living and dining areas articulated around spacious terraces, and service areas in perfect relation to the former. The deliberate verticality of the elevations (to which the disposition of the cladding tiles and wooden shutters contributes) helps to unify the volume and discourage any possible impression of a series of individual family houses piled on top of one another.

In the case of the "Les Cotxeres" complex by the same architects (paseo de Manuel Girona, 75; 1968-1973), the high density allowed in the planning regulations for the site of the old tram depot suggested, once again, a layout that would not result in excessive height, repeating solutions in the design of the plan previously tested in the Raset complex and elsewhere.

"Les Cotxeres" residential complex.

74
Banco Industrial de Bilbao — 1969-1973

Av. de la Diagonal, 468-472
Josep Maria Fargas Falp and Enric Tous Carbó, architects
Bus 6, 7, 15, 16, 17, 33, 34. Metro L3, L5 (Diagonal)

Without renouncing technological experimentation or the expressive potential this can make possible, in their design for this building Fargas and Tous sought, in contrast to the approach adopted in the Banca Catalana, an integration into the Ensanche in a manner that includes some of the constants of zone's urban fabric.

In effect, the most interesting exercise in this building is the attempt at combining the treatment of the facade as no more than an envelope (liberated from any load-bearing function by the structure of metal pillars and mixed girders, which further permits the large expanses of open space in the interior) with its capacity for integration into its urban surroundings. The outcome is an admirable curtain-wall (in the broad sense of the term) which has abandoned the pure plane to incorporate elements reminiscent of the traditional residential balcony (here, however, drawn horizontally), while the oxidized steel evokes the texture of stone.

On the ground floor is one of the branches of the Furest menswear shop designed by Federico Correa, opened in 1974. Not far from the BIB (now the Banco de Bilbao-Vizcaya) is the Caixa d'Estalvis i Pensions de Barcelona building (Av. Diagonal, 522-532; 1968-1973), in which the curtain-wall is screened by a sunscreen of adjustable vertical glass slats, the work of the architect Xavier Busquets Sindreu, who also designed the Sandoz office building (Gran Via de les Corts Catalanes, 766-768; 1971-1972).

The Caixa d'Estalvis i Pensions building.

75
Bonanova residential complex   1970-1973

Paseo de la Bonanova, 92
Oriol Bohigas, Josep Martorell and David Mackay, architects
Bus 22, 64, 66, 75, 94. FF.CC. Generalitat (Sarrià)

If, from the Casa del Pati on, the communal interior spaces assume a decisive significance in the residential architecture of the MBM team, starting in the late sixties there is a pronounced concern with exploiting to the full –for the benefit of the occupants– the relations between internal and external spaces (whether these be the central void of a city block redefined in function and conception, or those established by planning norms around the fringes of the new construction).

In the present case, to quote the architects themselves, "the urban planning regulations established for the entire zone a type of free-standing, high-density building that almost without exception configured the continuation of longitudinal blocks set perpendicular to the street, a circumstance which prevented the surplus spaces from acquiring their optimum expression and use. The greater width of this plot made it possible to organize two L-shaped buildings that delimited a series of free spaces: pedestrian access route, garage entrance, private-communal garden, swimming pool, etc.".

This new disposition duly became the most characteristic feature of this complex of 33 apartments in a wealthy residential neighbourhood, and the most significant contribution to the area's urban morphology.

Other instances of the team's exploitation of communal free spaces for the general good of the residents are the apartment buildings at c/ Rocafort, 242 bis-246 (1971-1973) and at c/ Eduard Conde, 50-52 (1975-1979).

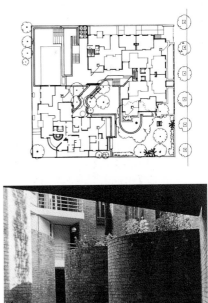

Les Escales Park residential complex

1967-1973

C/ Sor Eulàlia de Anzizu, 24
Josep Lluís Sert, Jackson & Associates
Estudi Anglada/Gelabert/Ribas (site supervision)
Bus 7, 75. Metro L3 (Palau Reial)

The return to the Catalan architectural scene of one of its leading figures of the years immediately prior to the Civil War failed to generate the resonance or the subsequent influence that might have been expected. Josep Lluís Sert –a mythic figure, lionized in his exile not only for his work but for his symbolic significance in those difficult, dramatic but nostalgic times– came back to Barcelona to produce a prestige residential complex and, a little later, to give material form to a cultural operation, the Fundació Miró, which the municipal authorities had shrewdly decided to support.

Nor did the strictly architectonic aspects of Sert's proposal for this residential complex generate great interest, in spite of the unquestionably effective and proper resolution of the general organization of the complex and its relations with its urban setting, or the calligraphy with which the whole was drawn. The prototype "duplex" apartments experimented with by Le Corbusier in the Immeubles-villas, which provided Sert with his inspiration

here, seemed far distant in time from the perspective of the contemporary Rationalism; either they had already served their purpose, or their moment had not yet come round again. And the incorporation of systems and materials taken from local construction tradition –with which Sert and the internationalist architects of his generation sought to "vernacularize" an architecture that had lost its capacity for evocation in its pursuit of the universal– was insufficient. The FAD award bestowed on the complex was, above all else, an act of historic reparation towards the architect.

77
Fundación Miró (Centro de Estudios de Arte Contemporanea)   1972-1974

Plaza de Neptú. Parque de Montjuïc
Josep Lluís Sert, Jackson & Associates (project)
Jaume Freixa Janáriz (project architect)
Estudio Anglada/Gelabert/Ribas (site supervision)
Bus 61. Metro L3 (Paral.lel). Funicular

The painter, sculptor and ceramicist Joan Miró wished that his native city should be home to the foundation that was to receive part of his work. The initiative was immediately welcomed by the municipal authorities, who proposed a site on the hill of Montjuïc, an emblematic location with a wealth of civic and recreational facilities. Sert, a personal friend of the artist, was commissioned to design the building; in doing so he turned to an earlier scheme of his own, the Fondation Maeght at Saint Paul de Vence (1959-1964). The outcome: a luminous building in white concrete, perfectly contrasted by the carefully maintained surrounding vegetation.

Alongside the entrance, a polygonal-plan tower –seen by some commentators as alluding to Gothic bell towers– accommodates the library and the functions room. And around the two courtyards, one with views over the city, the exhibition rooms are laid out in succession, with changes in level occasioned by the topography of the site. The rooms are lit from above, so that the facades have the appearance of hermetic, rigorously plane walls with barely a single opening or decoration, while the curving projections through which light enters give the exterior of the building its characteristic silhouette.

During 1987 and 1988, functional requirements made it necessary for the building to be extended. This extension, by the Catalan architect Jaume Freixa, who had worked with Sert on the original project, fully respects the formal and spatial qualities of the original.

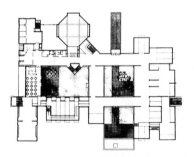

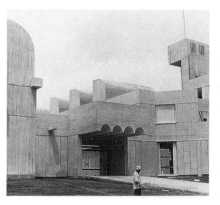

Instituto Francés

1972-1975

C/ Moià, 8
José Antonio Coderch de Sentmenat, architect
Bus 6, 7, 15, 27, 30, 33, 34, 58, 64

Coderch (no longer with Manuel Valls as a collaborator) proposed that the client renounce part of the usable area of the plot in order to provide the teaching facility with the optimum conditions in its siting in the city block, in both functional and representational terms. The outcome was the decision to occupy only the rear part of the plot at ground floor level –leaving space for a courtyard and landscaped area adjoining the street– and construct a seven-storey block whose expressive force derives entirely from the imposing volumetry and the eurhythmic sequence of a single type of vertically elongated opening that is repeated over all four elevations.

The opaque surfaces of the facades are, in consequence, a framework of vertical solids (which act to screen out the sun and ensure the privacy of the classrooms) cut across by the horizontal lines of the floor slabs, and clad with ceramic tiles set once again in a vertical arrangement. The metalwork detailing is flush with the exterior plane of the facade, thus unifying the surface.

In the original project, the top floor was to be enclosed by a blind wall, with the caretakers' residence behind it, looking onto the interior courtyard. This solution would undoubtedly have favoured the integral force of the composition, but the planning authorities objected. Coderch, obliged to perforate the parapet, opted to repeat –now with no other justification than that of preserving a sense of unity– the vertical opening, here traversed on the interior by a balustrade.

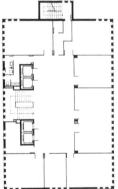

79
Escuela Thau

1972-1975

Carretera d'Esplugues, 49-53
Oriol Bohigas, Josep Martorell y David Mackay, architects
Bus 75. Metro L3 (Zona Universitària)

Reforms of the educational system are generally accompanied by a rethinking of school architecture. The highly effective work of the Ajuntament de Barcelona's cultural commission in the thirties was closely associated with Josep Goday's innovative architecture. The educational reforms following the restoration of democracy in 1978 have been provided with a homgeneous public architecture that nevertheless offers considerable formal diversity. Progress in education in Catalonia during the difficult years of the Franco dictatorship depended almost exclusively on private initiatives, and this circumstance, too, was reflected in architecture. The Escola Thau is an example of this.

The programme is developed in two three-storey buildings –one for infants and primary classes, the other for secondary classes– constructed on different levels to adapt to the topography, with the sloping terrain between them being used to provide a social and recreational area in the form of an amphitheatre. The distribution of the in-

terior and exterior spaces, and their interrelation, the treatment of the facades with curtain-walls and the concern with creating transparent, well-lit interiors are the essential elements which the architecture places in the service of active pedagogy. In 1986, a sports complex was constructed in the school grounds, designed by Josep M. Gutiérrez, Pere Riera and Jordi Fargas.

Another private facility designed by the MBM team at this time is the Clínica Augusta (c/ Madrazo, 8-10; 1971-1975).

Apartment building

1971-1974

C/ Treball, 197

José Antonio Martínez Lapeña and Elías Torres Tur, architects

Bus 40, 42, 43, 56, 544

The tower block, a cuboid with a rectangular plan, serves as a visual reference point for a district of poor quality –in terms of form and materials– housing, planned and built for the most part during the sixties. The high-rise contains eighty apartments distributed over sixteen floors. The apartments at either end of the building are single-level, while the two in the middle are developed over two levels, and this is revealed in the exterior composition of the elements on the facade, creating an attractively assymetrical play of voids and projections. The skin is of exposed brickwork, with large expanses of smooth blind wall at either end and on the north facade, in contrast to the projecting volumes of the glazed balconies concentrated on the south facade.

In the last days of the dictatorship, the most interesting architecture being constructed in Barcelona was, understandably, private apartment buildings. The first half of the seventies saw the construction of the buildings at c/ Tres Torres, 44-50, by Lluís Nadal Oller (1970-1974); at c/ Costa, 55-57, by Jo-sep Alemany and Josep Emili Hernández Cros (1971-1974); at c/ Tòquio, 2, by Josep Bonet and Cristian Cirici (1972-1974); at c/ Freixa, 11 and 13, by Santiago Balcells Gorina (1973-1974), and at c/ Duquesa d'Orleans, 1, by Emili Donato Folch (1973-1976). In nearby Sant Just Desvern, between 1970 and 1975 a housing cooperative commissioned Ricardo Bofill to construct the Walden 7 complex, referred to at the time as a "city in space", but today much degraded and in continual process of restoration.

House at c/ Tòquio, 2.

Building at c/ Treball, 197.

House at c/ Tres Torres, 44-50.

81
Frègoli building

1972-1975

C/ Madrazo, 54-56
Esteve Bonell Costa, architect
Bus 58, 64. FF.CC. Generalitat (Muntaner)

Ever since the rationalists first proclaimed the hygienic and therapeutic advantages –perhaps never fully elucidated– of laying out the domestic space over two levels, recourse to this distribution scheme has been a constant of architecture with a commitment to culture. Once its spatial possibilities and the aesthetic effectiveness of its manifestation on the facade had been demonstrated (these in all likelihood being the true reasons for its original use in the thirties), "duplex" apartments proliferated in seventies Barcelona, arguably exceeding the number of people willing to live in them.

In this building, Bonell committed himself unreservedly, exploring all of the interior and exterior possibilities of this type of housing. The asymmetry of the composition, the fragmentation of the volumes and the diversity of the different elements (sunscreens with adjustable slats, glazed galleries, metal balustrades) combine with the opacity of the top two floors –in a possibly somewhat ingenuous attempt at detaching them from the rest of the composition in order to "finish" the building at the same height as its neighbours– to

add up to a lot of risk factors for a facade that sought to keep faith with the interior. Fortunately, the talent of the architect was sufficient to make it work.

Esteve Bonell, while he was still a student, designed the apartment building at av. de Madrid, 142 (1969) with the architect Xosé M. Casabella, in which the agitated facade attempts, albeit here unsuccessfully, to escape from those mannerist tics that this project for the Frègoli building so skilfully transcends.

Apartment building

1971-1976

Av. del Coll del Portell, 52
Francesc Rius Camps, architect
Bus 24, 31, 32, 74

Alongside the vogue for the "duplex" model of apartment, the seventies were marked by a taste for split-level domestic interiors, particularly in the living and dining area, but the translation of these modes into more modest homes entailed certain risks. Steep, narrow stairs, unseen steps, unuseable corners could all produce inconvenience without guaranteeing any compensating spatial richness.

In this building, the architect assumed all of these risks without entirely getting around them, although he did succeed in profiting in the composition of the facades from this interior disposition of the apartments. However, the particular quality of this building perched on the side of a hill is derived from the use of one dominant material: structure, terraces, catwalks, part of the outer envelope and even the free-standing cylindrical volumes of the stairs and the lift are all executed in iron. The result asks to be considered not so much as deriving from a rationalization of the construction process as an interesting exercise in the skilful application of a given technological language.

In the contemporary apartment building at c/ Galileo, 281-285, by Helio Piñón Pallarés and Albert Viaplana Vea (1971-1976), the sacrifice of rationality for the sake of "originality" in the plan and certain formal results on the facades heralds the advent of the aestheticism that was to impose itself on so much of the architecture of the last quarter century, a position consistently upheld by these architects.

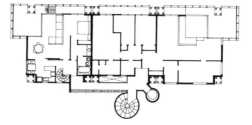

Apartment building at c/ Galileo, 281-285.

1978-2002

The death of General Franco in the last year of the third quarter of the century was of necessity to have a dramatic influence on the progress of architecture in Spain. The political and social renaissance that almost immediately ensued gave rise to a variety of phenomena which affected it directly. The results began to be apparent with the reform of the country's political structures, especially at the local level. We have therefore chosen to begin this chapter in 1978, the year that the new Constitution was approved, opening the doors to democracy.

These phenomena are: a new sensitivity to the past (monuments, sites, historic centres and complexes); a very considerable quantitative increase in the activity of the public sector (housing, services and amenities, urban reforms, etc.), and the incorporation into this endeavour of skilled professionals with a high level of architectural culture.

The old historic architecture
The first of these phenomena –which also sprang from other economic and cultural roots and concomitant factors– saw to it that a large number of the most significant works of this period bore some relation to historic architecture. It is to be regretted, however, that quantity was not always equalled by quality. The lack of any clear orientation in the theory and practice of restoration of monuments was very much in evidence throughout these years.

Confusions in relation to the concept of heritage (in some cases assessed more on the basis of economic potential than of cultural value; in others, its documentary essence subordinated to its architectonic qualities); the shortage of qualified professionals capable of thinking through the appropriate intervention in the historic monuments or urban fabric, the legacy of so many years of contempt and neglect for the culture of restoration, and the precarious situation of the mechanisms for the control, evaluation and distribution of resources under the new democratic authorities were amongst the causes of this general state of affairs.

In Barcelona, moreover, despite appearances to the contrary, this phenomenon was very limited in its scope. Successive democratic city councils, spellbound by the task of making the future a present reality, devoted insufficient attention to the past. The fragile mechanisms for conservation bequeathed by the distatorship were not brought up to date (in spite of the evident obsolescence of the aesthetic regulation of the Ensanche and the pressing need to extend the list of protected buildings) and the cultural evaluation of historic works of architecture was mediated by political and commercial interpretations of their significance to the community.

The result of all of this was that, while interventions in Barcelona's architectural heritage during this period were numerous (conversions of palaces and monasteries, the reconstruction of demolished masterpieces, the cleaning of facades and the rehabilitation of buildings of all kinds), there were very few restorations that could be described as scientific or even as properly respectful of the original.

Restoration of the Casa de Alturas. Víctor Argentí (1985-1989).

The new public architecture

At the same time, however, the democratization of political structures during this period also resulted in a greater public presence in all those activities relating to the city as a collective whole; actions made all the more urgently necessary by the deficits inherited from the previous regime. This made itself apparent in the spectacular increase in public-sector construction (schools, community centres, sports and cultural facilities, institutional and service buildings, parks, roads, urban spaces and so on).

Barcelona also experienced in this quarter century a circumstance of exceptional significance in this regard: the celebration of the 1992 Summer Olympic Games. This fact, of transcendent value in a city accustomed to refurbishing itself for such occasions, propitiated the profound and far-reaching process of urban reform that Oriol Bohigas had initiated even before the Olympic bid was first conceived. Barcelona was once again to be "the city of prodigies", as Eduardo Mendoza has called it.

At the same time, this renovation of political and administrative structures made it possible for these works of public architecture to be designed by architects with an interest in ensuring that their work was in line with the standards demanded by the new conditions. The reform of infrastructures and the architectural production occasioned by the transformation of the city were consequently able to attain a level of interest that made Barcelona a focus of international attention. The Horta cycle track by Bonell and Rius; the plaza dels Països Catalans by Piñón and Viaplana; the Collserola tower by Foster; the Bac de Roda bridge by Calatrava;

The regulation of the Ensanche. House at c/ Mallorca, 205 (1983-1984).

the Palacio Sant Jordi by Isozaki, and the new airport terminals by Bofill are, together with the Badalona sports pavilion by Bonell and Rius, illustrative examples of this outstanding public architecture evaluated in the context of an ambitious programme of urban reforms.

The hegemonic role –in both quantitative and cultural terms– of this paradigm public architecture during this period is evident in the selection of works presented on the pages that follow. In contrast to the two previous chapters, in which schemes for private clients predominate, in this third chapter publicly funded projects account for more than three quarters of the total.

Aestheticism as an attitude

In strictly disciplinary terms, the local architecture of this period was inhibited by its own contradictions. While, overall, it is characterized by a considerable level of creativity, it is also conditioned by the chronic persistence of certain vices and habits that date from some years earlier: the undervaluing of function and a knowledge of construction as key factors in shaping the project, and aestheticism as a design attitude.

The dissociation between design and utility is particularly damaging in

that this was an architecture, as we noted, supposedly in the service of the community. The dichotomy between project design and building techniques is at the same time a direct consequence of the approach to teaching practised in our architecture schools. It embodies, moreover, a patent contradiction: these were years of a manifest increase in the number of specialists (in structural design, in services, etc.) involved in the drawing up of these projects. But the dichotomy unquestionably exists, since in many cases the specialists' knowledge of construction was limited to "making possible" a design elaborated on the basis of this aestheticism as a primary design attitude.

For this reason, the result is very often a fragile and prematurely obsolete architecture, immune to certain stylistic influences proceding from outside the local context, and conceived more with a view to its reception within the specialized forums of professional debate than for the benefit of its users.

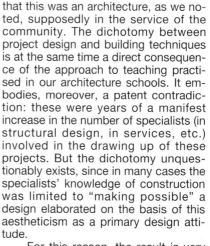

Hotel Podium. M. Bayarri, J. Gómez, J. A. Cordón, A. Canal.

Detail of the Olympic Village.

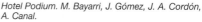

Badalona municipal sports pavilion. E. Bonell and F. Rius.

Post-Olympic architecture

The majority of the works commenced as part of the series of urban reforms undertaken on the occasion of the 1992 Summer Olympic Games were completed by 1993. Nevertheless, others were to continue throughout the entire period of the Atlanta Olympiad, while some even extended beyond the close of the Summer Olympic Games held in 1996. This is the case of the refurbishment of the Palau Nacional, constructed for the Barcelona International Exhibition of 1929, to house the restructured Museu Nacional d'Art de Catalunya, commenced in 1985. The building was subjected to a programme of major consolidation and remodelling, designed by the Italian architect Gae Aulenti and supervised on site by the Catalan architect Enric Steegman. The remodelling of this "palace" originally built for purely temporary use has received some severe criticism, particularly from the local population, in terms of both the intervention in the existing architecture and the treatment of its function as a museum.

Other actuations that significantly overstepped the bounds of Barcelona's Olympic period include the transformation of the old Casa de la Caridad, a historic building partly demolished to make way for the construction of the Museu d'Art Contemporani de Barcelona; the "Illa Diagonal" building; the Caja de Madrid building (Avda. Diagonal, 640, at the junction of Avda. Sarrià) by Josep Maria Fargas and Enric Tous, and the electrical energy transport control building in the Paral.lel by Salvador Pérez Arroyo. The Teatre Nacional de Catalunya, by Ricard Bofill, was completed in 1997, and the neighbouring Auditori, by Rafael Moneo, was opened early in 1999. Both of these public facilities are on the Plaça de les Arts.

During these post-Olympic years (1992-2000), public initiatives continued to play the leading role in the city's most interesting architectural ventures, thanks above all to the fact that the renewed impetus to provide Barcelona with satisfactory university facilities has been accompanied by an explicit commitment to maintaining a high level of quality in the design. Private enterprise has also been unusually active, especially in the new urban space of the former football stadium of R.C.D. Español and in the Diagonal Mar area, under the impetus of the holding of the World Forum of Cultures (Barcelona 2004).

World Trade Center, I.M. Pei, arch. (1999).

Les Corts thanatorium. Marina Salvador, arch. (1996)

Faculty of Communications Sciences. Universidad Ramon Llull. Dani Freixes, arch. (1996).

83
Escuela Técnica Superior de Arquitectura (extension) **1978-1982**

Av. de la Diagonal, 649
José Antonio Coderch de Sentmenat, architect
Estudio Coderch de Sentmenat
Bus 7, 75. Metro L3 (Zona Universitària)

The boom in the construction industry brought about by the economic growth of the sixties led to a widespread belief that architecture was a profession with a future. The resulting increase in the number of applicants to study architecture, attracted by the prospects, meant that the School of Architecture, then only fifteen years old, had to be expanded. With the extension agreed on, the architect chosen to design it was the person who had contributed most to the rebirth and the maintenance of the highest standards in Catalan architecture over the last twenty or thirty years, a highly intelligent decision at the start of a new phase in the history of architecture in Catalonia.

The extension, situated at the back of the existing building, is developed over two floors, stepped to adapt to the difference in level between the main vestibule and the street to the rear. The curving form of the plan reflects, as Coderch affirmed, the desire to orient the classrooms towards the gardens to the north. so that the students could "look outside and be diverted from time to time". The central class-rooms, which face south, are illuminated by way of courtyards providing direct and filtered light. The treatment of the exterior is resolved, as in earlier buildings by Coderch, with vertical ceramic tiles which adapt well to the sinuous outline of the walls.

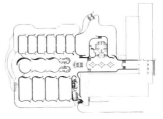

Basement floor plan.

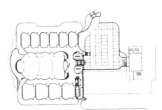

Ground floor plan.

Pi i Molist residential complex   **1978-1981**

C/ Doctor Pi i Molist, 39-63
Jordi Garcés Brusés and Enric Sòria Badia, architects
Bus 11, 12, 31, 32, 47, 50, 51, 77. Metro L5 (Virrei Amat)

The complex was constructed for the Instituto Nacional de la Vivienda, with a programme comprising 63 apartments measuring some 75 m², a garage and shops. It consists of two parallel rectangular blocks connected by a roofed central volume with a skylight, which accommodates the stairs. All of the rooms open to the exterior, either onto the street, onto the courtyard in the middle of the city block, or onto the central space, thus avoiding the need for light wells in the building itself.

The distribution scheme of the apartments stems from a desire to ensure the flexibility of the communal spaces where possible, so that these are separated by movable partitions. Only the bedrooms open onto the cen-tral space between the two blocks, in order to take advantage of its relatively low levels of noise and dirt. The perfectly plane facades, notably austere and simple in their composition, are of exposed brickwork.

85
Río de Janeiro residential complex 1978-1981

Av. del Río de Janeiro, (unnumbered); c/ Sanchis Guarner, 14-16, 7-9
Lluís Nadal Oller, architect
Bus 12, 73. Metro L4 (Lluchmajor)

The Patronato Municipal de la Vivienda municipal housing authority constructed this residential complex, intended to ease the shortage of low-cost housing in the north-eastern part of the city. The operation also involved the urban remodelling of the zone (35 hectares of land formerly occupied by the Sant Andreu railway station), so that the idea of the project was based on a desire to endow the built complex with its own urban character.

The entry into the complex passes between two eleven-storey tower blocks which flank a pedestrian street overlooked by the two lower, longitudinal five-storey blocks, with the pedestrian passage giving access to the apartments. The treatment of the facades is unitary, with smooth exterior walls of exposed brickwork and a regular and symmetrical rhythm in the openings in each of the buildings. The exterior spaces act as elements articulating communal activities while at the same time resolving the problem of the pronounced difference in level between the two ends of the plot.

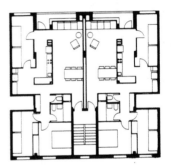

86
La Farigola del Clot E.G.B. primary school

1977-1980

C/ Hernán Cortés, (unnumbered)
Jordi Bosch Genover, Joan Tarrús Galter and Santiago Vives Sanfeliu, architects
Bus 18, 62, 92. Metro L1 (Clot)

The school was built by the Ajuntament de Barcelona, on a plot of land that had belonged to the Spanish state RENFE railway company. The building adopts a T-shaped plan, with the longer side accommodating the entrance porch, including administrative offices, and a broad corridor with a glazed roof which resolves much of the school's circulation. On either side of this axis are the multi-purpose rooms, which can be enlarged by moving back the large full-length windows which look onto the corridor. The transverse volume accommodates the classrooms, which are separated by sliding wooden panels to allow these spaces to be redistributed in different ways.

The school received the FAD Architecture Award 1980 in explicit recognition of the new level of quality that was beginning to establish itself in the public sector.

The same architects designed the El Sagrer public school, at c/ Costa Rica, 26 (1980-1983). A little later, between 1984 and 1986, the architects Ramon Artigues Codó and Ramon Sanabria Boix designed the Sant Joan de Ribera public school (c/ Aragó, 616).

87
Eduard Fontseré public school (La Teixonera)

1978-1982

C/ Farnés, 60; c/ Pantà de Tremp, (unnumbered)
Josep Emili Donato Folch and Uwe Geest, architects
Bus 19, 86

Within the new wave of public-sector architecture that came to the fore in the first years of the restored democracy, school buildings occupied a place of quantitative prominence. The La Teixonera public school was one of a number of facilities jointly funded and built by the Ayuntamiento de Barcelona and the Spanish Ministry of Education and Science in the late seventies, for the most part in economically depressed districts with a history of inadequate school provision.

The school is situated in an outlying area of the city, adjacent to the avinguda de la Vall d'Hebron, in a dense, chaotic urban context. The basic idea underlying the project was that new-build public interventions in districts lacking an established civic character "are obliged to signal with the greatest possible force and simplicity their desire to order and reconstruct the city landscape". The result here is a series of volumes articulated in such a way that the central construction, longitudinal and porticoed, serves as a containing wall against which are set, at one end, the triangular volume housing the multi-purpose hall that receives daylight by way of a central glazed column, and at the other, a rotunda for communal use which defines the school's playground.

Amongst other noteworthy school centres constructed around this time are the Colegio IPSI (c/ Comte Borrell, 243-249, by Josep Benedito, Jaume Llobet and Agustí Mateos; 1975-1978) and the Instituto L'Alzina (pasaje Salvador Riera, 2, by Gabriel Mora and Jaume Bach; 1978-1982).

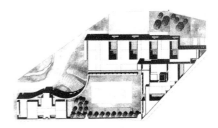

BD. Ediciones de Diseño shop (Casa Thomas)

1979

C/ Mallorca, 291

Studio PER. Cristian Cirici Alomar, architect

Bus 20, 21, 43, 544. Metro L3, L4, L5 (Diagonal, Verdaguer)

The shop is located on the ground and semi-basement floors of the Casa Thomas –constructed in 1895 by the architect Lluís Domènech Montaner– in the premises once occupied by the graphic arts business of the same name, which closed down in 1973. The remodelling divided the below-ground level into two spaces, one as a store and the other as a display area, the only part of the shop visible from the street. The exterior skin –a large sheet of plate glass– protects the original stained glass and the wrought iron railing of the upper level and reveals the double-height showcase window that serves to link the two floors and lies directly underneath the courtyard in the centre of the building, from which it receives daylight by way of a skylight.

This was regarded in its day as a pioneering piece of work, introducing a new approach to the act of intervening in the architectonic heritage, and was rewarded with the 1979 Premio Nacional de Restauración, in the year this award for restoration was first made.

Two other significant interventions in the city's architectonic patrimony at around this time were carried out by the architects Jordi Garcés and Enric Sòria: the remodelling of a 19th-century asylum to house the Museum of Science (c/ Teodor Roviralta, 55; 1979-1980), and the reform of the Palau Meca, at c/ Montcada, 19, to extend the Museo Picasso (1981-1986). This latter intervention generated controversy because some of the project decisions, and the speed with which the work was executed, were felt to have detracted from the historical and formal values of the original building.

In 1999 two new buildings were incorporated into the museum: the Mauri House and the Finestres House, likewise in the Calle Montcada. The design by Jordi Garcés also involved the dismantling of most of the interiors of the property so as to increase the amount of wall surface for exhibiting works of art.

The Museo de la Ciència.

89
Pabellón de la Merced.
Hospital de San Pablo   1979-1980

C/ Sant Antoni Maria Claret, 167
Antoni González Moreno-Navarro, Víctor Argentí Salvadó and
José Luis González Moreno-Navarro, architects
Bus 15, 19, 20, 45, 47, 50. Metro L5 (Hospital de Sant Pau)

The Pavellón de la Merced was the only building of the pavilion-type hospital complex designed by Lluís Domènech Montaner to survive to the end of the seventies without major modification, although by that time its physical deterioration called out for urgent attention, the response being a joint, coordinated intervention by the Ministry of Culture and the Hospital. The former took charge of the restoration of the exterior, and the latter the interior and the creation of a new department of Obstetrics.

The basic criteria in this intervention were: to restore the building to its original state as faithfully as possible, and promote a dialogue between the original construction and the –reversible– new elements. This dialogue was conceived as facilitating contemplation and understanding of Domènech's pa-

vilion without denying the new intervention its own values and expressive character. The installation within the central bay of new volumes to contain various medical functions, with the section and dimensions calculated to reveal and elucidate the original architecture, and the almost domestic treatment of the spaces for the mothers-to-be, in order to facilitate personal contact, are two of the most significant features of the intervention, which won a FAD Restoration award in 1980.

A FAD award also went, in 1983, to the adaptation by the architects Andreu Bosch, Lluís Cuspinera and Josep Maria Botey of the Ave Maria pavilion of the Casa de Maternitat de Barcelona to house the Generalitat de Catalunya's Ministry of Health.

"La Sedeta" school and community centre

1978-1983

C/ Sicília, 303; c/ Indústria
Ricard Fayos Molet, Pere Giol Draper, Ferran Llistosella Vidal and
F. Xavier Llistosella Vidal, architects
Bus 15, 20, 45, 47. Metro L5 (Sagrada Família), L4 (Joanic)

The restoration and reutilization of old buildings of architectonic, historical or symbolic interest was a priority objective of the new democratic city authorities, and at the same time an effective strategy for tackling the deficit of public facilities inherited from the previous regime.

The conversion of the La Sedeta textile factory as a school and community centre is an interesting example of this process of architectural recycling, skilfully and effectively resolved. The building occupies almost half an En-

sanche city block, with the two manufacturing wings aligned along c/ Indústria and c/ Sicília now containing the EGB and BUP (primary and secondary) schools and the community centre. In order to conserve the original aspect of the complex for the benefit of the district as a whole, the facade of the building fronting onto c/ Sant Antoni Maria Claret has been retained; behind it are the schools' recreation and play areas and the open plaza created in the interior of the courtyard in the middle of the block.

Another example of the rehabilitation of an old industrial building for use as a community facility can be found in the Les Corts public school (c/ Eugeni d'Ors, 2), the conversion of the former FIAT workshops by the architects Sergi Godia, Juli Laviña, Josep Urgell, Pilar de la Villa, Pere Aixas and Xavier Gomà and the clerk of works Joan Ardèvol (1979-1981).

Les Corts public school.

91
Les Cotxeres de Sants community centre 1977-1984

C/ Sants, 79-81; c/ Olzinelles, 19; pl. Bonet i Muixí
Ricardo Pérdigo Nardiz, Antoni Pujol Niubó and
Tomàs Rodríguez Coll, architects
Bus 56, 57. Metro L1, L5 (Plaça de Sants)

During the seventies, popular pressure to have obsolete infrastructures and industrial buildings in residential neighbourhoods converted for use as community amenities was a frequent feature of Barcelona life. The campaign mounted by local political, social and cultural groups in the district of Sants to reclaim for the public good the old tram depot, the "cotxeres", was one successful example of this.

A sketch-design competition was held in 1977, and in 1978 the Ayuntamiento de Barcelona commissioned the winning team to draw up the final construction project, taking in the conversion of not only the old tram depot but its immediate surroundings, the key features of which were the former carriage halt, the tram depot itself, the church of Santa Maria de Sants and an old farmhouse known as the Casa del Rellotge.

The scheme set out to take the fullest possible advantage of the existing spaces, both buildings and squares, obtaining the maximum social and functional utility without undermining their symbolic or civic value. The complex was subsequently extended with the addition of the Josep Miracle building on the corner of c/ Olzinelles and the plaza Bonet i Muixí (then the plaza de Málaga), to be used as a senior citiens' residence and other social services. The project for the rehabilitation of this latter building was carried out between 1986 and 1988 by Ricardo Pérdigo and Tomàs Rodríguez.

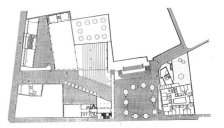

Plaza dels Països Catalans   1981-1983

(Sants railway station)
Helio Piñón Pallarés and Albert Viaplana Vea, architects
(with Enric Miralles, architect)
Bus 27, 30, 43, 109, 544. Metro L3, L5 (Sants-Estació)

The square in front of Barcelona's new main railway station was in fact no more than a residual urban space bordered by buildings of scant interest and major roads. Any attempt at tackling its urban remodelling was considerably hampered, moreover, by the nature of the soil, with railway tunnels running just below the surface, prohibiting the introduction of elements above a certain weight or deep-rooting vegetation such as trees. in view of these considerations, the fundamental idea was to endow the space with a monumentality and expressive force capable of minimizing the surroundings and introducing a poetic note into this urban sector.

The architects introduced a series of metal objects –more sculptural than architectonic– dispersed across the carpet of pink granite that forms the paving: the pergola with its undulating roof, the ample 15 metre-high canopy, the double row of inclined fountains, the barriers, the lighting elements, etc. The design solution has been justified as the product of conceptual discourses or metaphors, although the general popular perception, little accustomed to thinking in such categories, continues to regard this space as a paradigm of the "plaza dura", the hard square, as opposed to the green or landscaped square, within the terms of an absurd polemic then raging in the city.

The plaza, 1983 FAD prize-winner, was first refurbished in 1991-1992. The same architects also designed the Parque del Besòs (ronda de Sant Raimon de Penyafort, c/ Cristòfol de Moura; 1982-1987), in a poorly maintained peripheral suburb.

93
Frègoli II apartment building
1981-1983

C/ Brusi, 19

Esteve Bonell Costa, architect

Bus 16, 17, 27, 30. FF.CC. Generalitat (Plaça Molina-Sant Gervasi)

Many of what were to emerge as the characteristic features of the architectural language of the eighties were already present in this apartment building which, belying its appearance as a private family house, contains four "triplex" apartments, two of them opening onto the street, the other two onto the courtyard in the interior of the city block, in a distribution designed to compensate for the limited dimensions of the plot. The street facade is finished with bush-hammered artificial stone, while the rear facade, which overlooks the garden, is of exposed brickwork. The accesses –vestibule and stairs– are finished in teak and white marble.

The development of the apartments over three floors organized around a central service core and stairway is also a feature of the apartment building at c/ Sant Cugat del Vallès, 1-3, by Francesc Rius Camps (1979-1981), crowned by an attic-conservatory to take advantage of solar energy. Also dating from 1981 is the apartment building at c/ Bertran, 67, by Carles Ferrater Lambarri, which rigorously pursues the duplex organization so clearly manifested on the exterior, and the Casa Olèrdola, at plaza Olèrdola, 3, by Jaume Bach and Gabriel Mora.

Casa Olèrdola.

117

Velodromo de Horta cycle track   1983-1984

Paseo de la Vall d'Hebron; paseo de Castanyers
Esteve Bonell Costa and Francesc Rius Camps, architects
Bus 27, 73, 76, 85. Metro L3 (Montbau)

The building is essentially a shallow, semi-sunken cylinder, the untreated outer skin of which alternates opaque stretches of brickwork and sequences of well-spaced pillars, with the whole perimeter crowned by a cornice in the form of a simple yet imposing horizontal disk. The circular form of this outer skin generates free spaces between it and the tiered seating around the outside of the wooden cycle track; these free spaces, unroofed as the track is, serve the access and circulation needs of up to 4,000 spectators. Beneath these spaces, in the interior of the cylinder, are the athletes changing rooms and services, with their own independent entrance.

The main access to the complex is by way of a broad flight of steps that leads up to a plaza surrounded by olive trees, and presided over by a three-dimensional visual poem by Joan Brossa. A second and larger plaza on the level of the upper part of the cylinder functions as an assembly area in front of the spectators' entrance. The tall angular lighting towers typical of sports stadiums rise up over the building and reinforce its intentionally monumental quality in a zone which at that time had a somewhat precarious urban character.

The state of conservation of the building, despite its status as 1984 FAD prize-winner, is far from ideal, perhaps partly on account of inadequate maintenance, and partly in consequence of the original construction work, which suffered considerably from the customary mismanagement of the public-sector architecture of the early 80s.

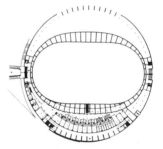

95
Casa Pascual i Pons
(La Catalana de Seguros)   1984

Paseo de Gràcia, 2-4; ronda de Sant Pere, 1; c/ Casp, 2-4
Reform and restoration: Oriol Bohigas, Josep Martorell, David Mackay,
Miquel Espinet y Antoni Ubach, architects; Lluís Pau, interior designer
Bus 16, 17, 22, 47. Metro L1, L2, L3; FF.CC. Generalitat (Catalunya)

This neo-Gothic palace, constructed during 1890 and 1891 by Enric Sagnier, had undergone numerous reforms over the years, to the great detriment of its original aspect. In 1984, with the refurbishment of the building as head office of an insurance company, it was decided to recover that original appearance. The spire of the tower on the chamfered corner of c/ Casp, mutilated in the sixties, was reconstructed and the facades were restored. In the interior, the main entrance to the house at no. 2 was also restored, as was the first floor, which had best conserved the quality of its public rooms. The building's new function made it necessary to construct a new well for the vertical circulation, and add a set-back volume under the new roof and a line of windows beneath the eaves. The scheme won the FAD Restoration award in 1984, the last time the award was made.

Other interventions in listed buildings at this time are the restoration of the Casas Xifré, at paseo de Isabel II, 8-14, directed by the architect Víctor Argentí Salvadó (1983-1985), and that of the Manning courtyard of the Casa de la Caridad, at c/ Montalegre, 7, by Andreu Bosch, Josep Maria Botey and Lluís Cuspinera (1985-1986). Also from this period is the reconstruction of the monument to Doctor Robert in the centre of the plaza de Tetuan (dismantled and removed from the plaza Universitat in 1939), carried out between 1976 and 1985.

Plaza de Sóller

1984

Josep Maria Julià Capdevila, Josep Lluís Delgado
Espallargas, Andreu Arriola Madorell and
Carme Ribas Seix, architects
Bus 11, 12, 31, 32, 47, 50, 51, 77

The square, a rectangle flanked by roads and buildings of little interest, in effect defines itself, in the words of the architects, "creating its own perimeter by means of the architecture, which establishes itself by balancing the six metre difference in level between the upper and lower extremes, thus forming a great tablet that projects out over the natural level of the terrain and creating a submerged side".

The space is divided into one zone with the character of a porticoed square, with services inside the porch, and another zone with the character of a park, delimited by side walls and a railing along the upper part. Between these two zones is a pond, out of which emerges the marble sculpture "Homenatge a les Illes" (Homage to the Islands) by Xavier Corberó, which had to be restored in 1990 as a result of the vandalism of the square.

Another equally interesting, and equally degraded, urban space from the same period is the plaza del Peu del Funicular, adjoining the avinguda de Vallvidrera. The steeply sloping topography of this square, laid out by the architect Josep Antoni Llinàs Carmona, required an intervention based on containing walls supporting an elevated platform, with flights of steps and a continuous bench backing onto them.

97
Plaza del Sol   1982-1985

Jaume Bach Núñez and Gabriel Mora Gramunt, architects
Bus 22, 24, 28, 39. Metro L3 (Fontana). FF.CC. Generalitat (Gràcia)

The intervention in this square was part of a more ambitious operation commissioned by the municipal authorities, involving the architects in remodelling various other squares in the district of Gràcia (in addition to the plaza del Sol, these were the Virreina, Trilla, Diamant and Raspall squares) as key elements in the urban configuration of the old town and still today essential spaces in the social and civic fabric of the lives of the people of Gràcia.

In the plaza del Sol, the need to construct an underground car park –the access ramp of which is situated on the west side– made it necessary to raise the original level and resolve the connection with the lower level by means of a linear set of steps that adapts to the topography of the site. The new surface, a continuous pavement of flags, and the boundaries created by the line of trees configure the form and character of the space and keep traffic other than service vehicles out of the square.

In all five squares, the elements of furniture were purpose-designed. Sculpture and fountains were also used, but without jeopardizing the traditional and individual character of each one.

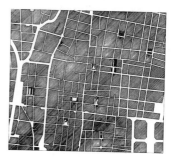

Parque de la España Industrial   1981-1985

C/ Sant Antoni, (unnumbered); c/ (Muntadas)
Luis Peña Ganchegui and Francesc Rius Camps, architects
Bus 27, 30, 43, 109, 544. Metro L3, L5 (Sants-Estació)

The park owes its existence, as in the case of the Les Cotxeres community centre in Sants, to local pressure, which persuaded the authorities to convert this site in Sants –formerly the Vapor Nou factory– for public recreational use. The "Casa del Mig" and a few plane trees flanking an avenue are surviving testimony to the original industrial complex.

The morphology of the terrain suggested an intervention in which the various elements –architecture, landscaping and sculpture– would be interrelated and at the same time dispersed in distinct zones, creating a harmonious space, both open and closed, a park-cum-salon where water is the dominant presence. The towers separating it from the more aggressive neighbouring environment of Sants railway station and the roads busy with traffic form a virtual wall which then gives way to the terraced steps leading down to the pond, in pedestrian itineraries that link together the various different zones. The park is peopled with sculptures by Enric Casanovas, Manuel Fuxà, Antoni Alsina, Anthony Caro, Andrés Nagel, Josep Pérez "Peresejo" and Pablo Pa-

lazuelo which "stimulate the imagination and poetic evocation", in the words of the architect Peña Ganchegui.

Not far from here (c/ Tarragona-c/ Aragó) is the Joan Miró park (Parque de l'Escorxador) designed by the architects Beth Galí, Màrius Quintana, Antoni Solanas and Andreu Arriola (1980-1982) on the site once occupied by a municipal slaughterhouse. On one side of the park is the Biblioteca Joan Miró public library (1989-1991), by Galí, Quintana and Solanas.

Parque de l'Escorxador. Sculpture by Joan Miró.

99
Parque de la Creueta del Coll   **1981-1987**

Av. de la Mare de Déu del Coll, (unnumbered)
Oriol Bohigas, Josep Martorell and David Mackay, architects
Bus 25, 28. Metro L3 (Vallcarca)

In laying out the park, the architects took full advantage of a disused quarry on this site, first allocated for use as a city park in the regional Plan Comarcal for Barcelona in 1953.

The exceptional morphology of the terrain was conducive to the basic idea that the project should establish two clearly differentiated zones: one on the north side, laid out as a wooded park equipped for children's play activities, with picnic, recreation and physical exercise areas; the other, to the south, ordered as a city park, with a strong emphasis on its designed elements, constituting a sequence of spaces suitable for both structured and unstructured play, sports of various kinds, and large gatherings of people celebrating local festivals and other public occasions.

This southern sector contains the large plaza, the lake and the flights of steps and esplanades of the amphitheatre, which connect with it by way of gently sloping paths, creating itineraries of great beauty, presided over by three large sculptures: one by Ellsworth Kelly, at the entrance; another at one end of the stretch of water, by Eduardo Chillida, and the third, on the summit of the hill, by Roy Lichtenstein.

Other urban parks laid out on former industrial sites during the early eighties include the Parque del Clot, by the architects Daniel Freixes, Vicente Miranda and Victor Argentí (1982-1986), and the Parque de la Pegaso, in c/ Sagrera, designed by Enric Batlle and Joan Roig (1982-1986).

Parque del Clot.

123

Gardens of the Vil.la Cecília   1982-1986

C/ Santa Amèlia, 29-33; c/ Eduard Conde; c/ Trinquet
José Antonio Martínez Lapeña y Elías Torres Tur, architects
Bus 6, 16, 34, 66, 70, 74. Metro L3 (Maria Cristina). FF.CC. Generalitat (Sarrià)

The gardens belonging to an old mansion, the Vil.la Cecília, which is now occupied by the Centro Cívico de Sarrià community centre, were extended with the incorporation of part of the gardens of a neighbouring property, the Quinta Amèlia, that had been left isolated from the house and the rest of the grounds when the road, the c/ Santa Amèlia, was built.

The classical layout of the old gardens of the Vil.la Cecília was modified, and a zone of discontinuous labyrinthine paths created, purposely cut across by lines of trees in order to oblige the visitor to discover each of the gardens' series of different spaces.

The furniture elements, the sculptural objects, the lampposts and the gates, together with the wall flanking the channel of water that serves as a frame for the sculpture of the drowned woman (a realist work by Francisco López Hernández), all reveal the creative capacity and design strengths these architects can bring to the execution of a wholly new project. This was the first garden to be awarded a FAD Architecture prize (1986).

101
Fossar de la Pedrera   **1983-1986**

C/ de la Mare de Déu del Port, (unnumbered). Montjuïc
Elisabeth Galí Camprubí and Màrius Quintana Creus, architects
Bus 9, 38, 72, 109

The pit of an old stone quarry used as a communal grave at the end of the Civil War in 1939 provides the inherently monumental framework for a commemorative and symbolic place of remembrance dedicated to the victims of that bitter conflict, resolved with a minimal architectonic intervention.

The itinerary commences with a twisting path that approaches the quarry at a tangent and culminates, by way of a flight of steps, in a grove of cypresses amongst which are stone pillars engraved with the names of the people shot here by Franco's troops in 1939. This point marks the beginning of a great curving esplanade of grass, framed by the sheer wall of the quarry and a linear walkway delimited by a pergola that leads up to the mausoleum of the president of the Generalitat de Catalunya, Lluís Companys, shot here in 1940.

The varied treatment of the paving, in different materials, serves to divide the itinerary into zones that are at the same time marked by the vertical elements that populate the landscape.

Via Júlia

1982-1986

Josep Maria Julià Capdevila and
Bernardo de Sola Susperregui, architects
Bus 11, 12, 31, 32, 47, 50, 51, 73, 76, 77.
Metro L4 (Lluchmajor, Roquetes)

The urbanistic reforms undertaken by the new democratic city council, conceived and directed by Oriol Bohigas, had the fundamental objective of regenerating the urban fabric of the city's outlying districts, which had suffered most from the haphazard approach of the previous period. One aspect of the new strategy was to promote the urban vitality of these districts in themselves and improve their communications links. Another and complementary strategy was what was referred to as the "monumentalization" of the peripheral districts, with the idea of endowing them with a level of urban design (including the specifically distinctive monumental elements) comparable with that of the city centre.

The intervention in the Via Júlia, a major axis of the Nou Barris district, set out to accomplish these objectives, some of them technical (urban structure, infrastructures and facilities), some more concerned with attaching new meanings to spaces, through the design of new street furniture or the introduction of sculptural elements, such as the piece *Els altres catalans* (The other Catalans) by Sergi Aguilar, or the column

of light, *Torre Favència*, by Antoni Rosselló Til.

Further examples of this policy of urban renewal can be seen in the reforms of the Av. de Gaudí (Màrius Quintana, 1982-1985), of the Av. Río de Janeiro (Paloma Bardají and Carles Teixidó, 1986-1989), of the Rambla de Prim (Javier San José Marqués, 1st stretch; Pedro Barragán, 2nd stretch; 1990-1992), of the plaza del General Moragues (Olga Tarrasó Climent, 1985-1987), and of the environs of the Rovira tunnel (Màrius Quintana, south sector; Manuel Ribas Piera, north sector).

103
Moll de la Fusta-Paseo de Colom 1983-1987

Manuel de Solà-Morales Rubió, architect
Bus 14, 16, 17, 18, 36, 45, 57, 59, 64
Metro L3 (Drassanes), L4 (Barceloneta)

The urban design of a quay in the old port, lying alongside a traditional promenade connecting two squares, set out to establish a link between the city and the sea, while at the same time serving as a platform for a series of traffic routes. The scheme identifies three different zones: the first, running along the facades overlooking the sea, is formed in part by the old palm-lined promenade and a lane for slow-moving local traffic and city services; the second, by the water's edge, a granite-cobbled esplanade planted with an orderly arrangement of palm trees, provides an exclusively pedestrian social area; the third, separating the other two, is a raised platform which accommodates the architectural elements (café-bars and pergolas). The underground level beneath this contains rapid transit lanes and car parks.

The connection between the three zones is more virtual than real on account of the differences in level and the traffic lanes, while the combination of languages –the 19th-century romanticism of the furniture, the formalism of the café-bars, the folk vernacular of the Dutch-style bridges– undermines any sense of overall intention in the design.

Other contemporary exercises in urban remodelling, equally mixed in their fortunes, include the plaza de la Mercè (Rosa M. Clotet Juan, Ramon Sanabria and Pere Casajoana, 1983); the squares of Basses de Sant Pere and Sant Agustí Vell (Rafael de Cáceres, 1982-1984), and the paseo de Picasso (Roser Amadó and Lluís Domènech, 1981-1983).

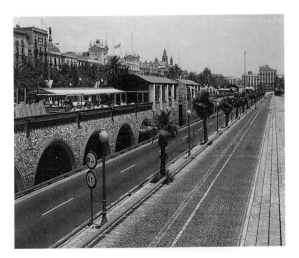

Bac de Roda bridge

1984-1987

C/ Felip II; c/ Bac de Roda
Santiago Calatrava Valls, architect and engineer
Bus 33, 34, 35, 43, 71, 544. Metro L5 (Navas)

The new bridge designed for the city council by the Valencian architect and engineer addressed two fundamental objectives: to establish connection –pedestrian and vehicular– between two districts separated by the railway line (an area intended for conversion into a park), and to create an outstanding landmark capable of bestowing significance on the rundown urban landscape.

The bridge, 128 metres long with a span of 45 metres, has a steel structure composed of two pairs of identical parabolic arches, the elements of each pair drawing together as they ascend, and opening out at the bottom to acommodate the footpaths. Four series of cables are suspended from these arches to support the stairs which lead up from the park and future railway station. The architects Pedro Barragán, Bernardo de Sola and Olga Tarrasó collaborated in the proyect, which received the 1987 FAD Archi-

tecture award, the first time the prize was given to a work of engineering.

Santiago Calatrava also designed the supports for the lane indicators over the Av. Diagonal between the plaza de Francesc Macià and the Esplugues de Llobregat bridge.

The bridge that carries c/ Cristòfol de Moura over the river Besòs in the neighbouring town of Sant Adrià de Besòs is the work of Enric Batlle Durany and Joan Roig Duran, from 1986-1988.

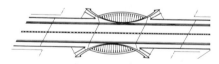

105
Arquitecte Josep M. Jujol
public school   1983-1987

C/ Riera de Sant Miquel, 41
Jaume Bach Núñez and Gabriel Mora Gramunt, architects
Bus 16, 17, 22, 24, 25, 28, 31, 32. FF.CC. Generalitat (Gràcia)

In their efforts to reduce the shortage of public schools, on certain occasions the municipal authorities opted to take over and convert an existing building of evident monumental value for educational use as a means of guaranteeing its conservation. Within the old fabric of Gràcia, the Modernista industrial bays of the Talleres Mañach, designed by Josep Maria Jujol (1916-1922) were faced with an uncertain future in private hands, and this resulted in their rehabilitation as a school facility.

The new building maintains the existing street alignment, onto which it gives a plane, stone-clad facade in which the striking doorway in the form of a semi-circular arch with a soldier-course brickwork archivault is a dominant element. The one-time workshop area is now the school playground.

A good example of a school complex constructed as an annex to an existing building is the Dolors Monserdà public school at Av. de Vallvidrera, 9, designed by Antoni de Moragas Spa (1986-1988); the integration of a new-built public facility into the urban grid of the Cerdà Ensanche can be seen in the Antoni Balmanya public school at c/ Freser, 103, and Sant Antoni Maria Claret, by the architects Esteve Terradas and Robert Terradas (1987-1988).

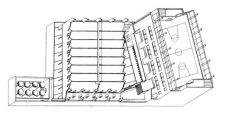

Seat of the Diputació de Barcelona
(Can Serra)   1985-1987

Rambla de Catalunya, 126; av. de la Diagonal
Federico Correa Ruiz and Javier Garrido Lagunilla, architects
Bus 6, 7, 15, 16, 17, 33, 34. Metro L3, L5 (Diagonal). FF.CC. Generalitat (Provença)

The protracted discussions between the owners of the Casa Serra (designed and built by Puig Cadafalch between 1903 and 1908, and extended by J. M. Pericas after the Civil War as a private school) and the Administration concluded with the demolition of the volume facing onto the Diagonal, the conservation of the part of the building forming the chamfered corner, and the construction of a new volume behind this to provide the agreed surface area.

Commissioned by the municipal authorities, Federico Correa drew up a detailed study of the city block that included the design of the new building, finished with a curtain-wall, and conceived more with a view to its integration with the existing architecture of the Diagonal than its relationship with the conserved part of Can Serra, behind which it rises up, making contact by means of an elevated passageway over a narrow side street. The cylindrical turrets on the corners of the new volume, replicating those of the house on the chamfered corner opposite, built by J. M. Pericas in 1917, the balustrades and other details in the finishing all seek integration with the building's surroundings.

Once the site and building permission had been obtained by the provincial Diputación, Correa completed his project and designed the assembly room and other interior spaces. The architect Javier Garrido played a decisive role in the supervision of the work on site. The new complex was inaugurated on April 22nd, 1987.

At this time the Correa-Milá team constructed a facsimile of the house at paseo de Gràcia, 80, making certain modifications to the original –which was demolished– by master builder Rafael Guastavino.

107
Baró de Viver group
of apartments

1985-1988

Paseo de Santa Coloma, (unnumbered)
Josep Emili Donato Folch, architect
Bus 35, 203. Metro L1 (Baró de Viver)

In 1984 the Patronat Municipal de l'Habitatge undertook the total renovation, in urban design and building, of this district of poor-quality housing. The fact of operating within a section of the urban fabric with no clear identity determined a dynamic approach based on structuring the new neighbourhood around a large, uni-directional public space which Donato, the architect, dubbed "Urban Salon". This space, which contains infrastructure and facilities, provides the functional and morphological support for the complex, which is organized as a series of blocks with three apartments in a split-level layout, abutting on one another in such a way that on the exterior elevation they present a smooth uniform plane and in

the interior follow an indented rhythm from top to bottom. The architect has remarked on the relationship this model has with the Viennese Hof, the Anglo-Saxon cluster and the Andalusian corrala, and which in Barcelona invites a reading as a possible updating of the courtyard in the centre of the Cerdà city block. "In all of these models the common theme", Donato observes, "expresses the primordial action of confining a portion of natural open space by means of the construction of limits that protect it from the outside and are at the same time a material and symbolic affirmation of the process of urban appropriation of territory and space."

Other contemporary operations in this line include the group of apartments at Nostra Senyora del Port, 190 - c/ Alts Forns, by Jordi Balari Muñoz and Albert Bastardes Porcel (1984-1987), and the complex at Gran Via de les Corts Catalanes, 944-980, by the architects Jordi Bosch, Joan Tarrús and Santiago Vives (1987).

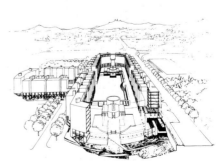

Guàrdia Urbana police station 1985-1988

La Rambla, 43

Ramon Artigues Codó and Ramon Sanabria Boix, architects

Bus 14, 18, 38, 59. Metro L3 (Liceu)

The site was originally occupied by the Colegio de Sant Angelo, constructed in 1593 and rebuilt in 1786-1790, of which only the cloister remains: incorporated into the new building and treated as an element of architectonic furniture, this cloister is now protected by a glazed roof. The exterior elevations of the new building express its public and representative character, clearly differentiating it from the apartment blocks on either side. The plan is developed in an L-shaped arrangement, and the rear facade, finished with an aluminium facing, opens onto an interior courtyard overlooked by old, poorly conserved residential buildings.

The series of interventions carried out by the Administration in the old central Ciutat Vella district, renewing the housing stock and installing new amenities and services, has produced a number of other interesting constructions: the apartment building at c/ Nou de la Rambla, 39-43, designed by Joan Arias, Luis Pérez de la Vega and Enric Torrent (1985-1988); the building at 73-79 of the same street, with its entrance at c/ Om, 1, by the Correa-Milá studio (1989-1990); the complex at c/ Om, 3-15, and Arc del Teatre, 48-52, by Jordi Bosch, Joan Tarrús and Santiago Vives (1989-1990); the Casa del Mar, at c/ Albareda, 1, by Oriol Tintoré (1989-1992), and the building for the Universitat Pompeu Fabra, at La Rambla, 30, by Josep Benedito and Jaume Llobet (1990-1992).

109
Centro de Arte Santa Mònica   1985-1989
La Rambla, 7

Helio Piñón Pallarés and Albert Viaplana Vea, architects

Bus 14, 18, 38, 59, 91. Metro L3 (Drassanes)

This 17th-century convent, with various later additions and modifications, had a series of new elements introduced into its baroque cloister –making it possible to manipulate the structural, functional and ambient characteristics of the building– in order to create an exhibition space. On the exterior, an access ramp-cum-terrace –with steel pillars and a floor of wooden planking– is set against the main facade. On the side facade, a very high portico or canopy acts as the nexus between new volume and conserved convent building. Alongside the main facade, separated by a perpendicular wall that delimits the accesses and functions of the two buildings, is the new facade of the church of Santa Mònica, with a great oculus as a rosette.

Some architecture critics have viewed this scheme as a paradigm of modern intervention in the architectonic heritage. Others, more closely involved with the field of monumental restoration, have expressed reservations as to whether a building of such slight architectural potency is capable of sustain-

ing so forceful an intervention without detriment to the original qualities ostensibly conserved or the new design. The issue thus raised is whether it might not have been more effective to have eliminated some of the elements added to the original structure over the centuries –apparently conserved for no other reason than to lessen the confusion created by this latest intervention– or even to have demolished the old convent and constructed an entirely new building, a task for which these architects are far more eminently qualified.

Plaza del Fossar de les Moreres   1988-1989

C/ Santa Maria, s/n
Carme Fiol Costa, architect
Bus 14, 16, 17, 40, 45, 51, 59, 64. Metro L4 (Jaume I)

The creation of a square in this marginal space opposite the side facade of the basilica of Santa Maria del Mar involved the demolition of a group of near-derelict buildings and the removal of the covered bridge or raised passageway that linked the church and the vice-regal palace of the Virrei, constructed in 1875.

The operation set out to commemorate the victims of the siege of Barcelona in 1714 by the troops of Felipe V, who are traditionally believed to be buried on this spot; an act of homage called for by various groups and associations. The symbolic aspect was thus a key consideration in the project design, which was also concerned to create a space for recreational use.

The scheme set out to satisfy both of these demands. On the boundary between square and street, a low wall of red granite bears a dedicatory inscription to the martyrs of the historic conflict by Serafí Pitarra, effectively focussing remembrance without melodrama or pathos, qualities alien to the Barcelonese character. The concave surface that slopes down towards the wall is paved in brick, laid in triangular segments to converge at the lowest point of the square, and bordered by the existing paving of Montjuïc sandstone, affording a space in which people can stroll, play or rest, and, on appropriate occasions, assemble for acts of remembrance or popular demonstrations. Three mulberry trees serve to reinforce the symbolic value of the memorial, which was inaugurated on September 11th, 1989.

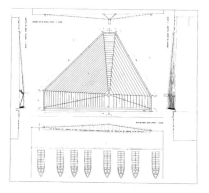

111
Parque de la Estació del Nord   1985-1991

C/ Nàpols; c/ Almogàvers; c/ de la Marina
Andreu Arriola Madorell, Carme Fiol Costa and
Enric Pericas Bosch, architects; Beverly Pepper, sculptress
Bus 6, 40, 42, 141. Metro L1, L2 (Arc de Triomf, Marina)

As part of the reorganization of the railway network –consigning the Estació del Nord to disuse– a new tunnel was constructed alongside the facade of the old passenger terminal (built in 1861 by the architect Andrés i Puigdoller), which was left partially submerged by the inclined plane of the new paving. Other sectors of the station environs also suffered as a result of the operation.

In order to rectify this situation, it was decided to lay out a park that would incorporate, or at least camouflage, these unfortunate accidents. The park was also to serve to link together a series of proposed interventions in this part of the city (the remodelling of the station, the new Archivo de la Corona d'Aragó, sports facilities, etc.). The space was to constitute a park-sculpture in which the modelling of the terrain would play a key part. This is divided into three sectors, each with its own focus of interest: the sculpture "Cel caigut" (Fallen sky), a low hill combining a "trencadis" ceramic mosaic and a carpet of grass; the "Espiral Arbrada" (Spiral of Trees), with its line of radially ordered trees opening up to form a spiral, and the ceramic walls of the c/ Almogàvers access.

Betwen 1986 and 1987 the architects Andreu Arriola and Carme Ribas Seix remodelled the Torre de les Aigües courtyard (c/ Roger de Llúria, 56), the project setting out to create a landscaped public space in the interior of a city block dominated by a tall water tower in the heart of the Cerdà Ensanche.

Facade for an apartment building   1987-1990

C/ Provença, 419-431; c/ Sardenya, 322
Joan Pascual Argenté, architect
Bus 19, 34, 43, 44, 50, 51, 54, 544. Metro L5 (Sagrada Família)

Municipal concern with maintaining an approved standard of quality in the design of the facades of new constructions on sites considered strategically important for the definition of the urban landscape resulted in the appearance around the city of a number of cases of dichotomous architecture. The developers would have their own architects design the building except for the facade, which would be entrusted to particular architects whose work was known to be in favour with the city bureaucracy.

In the case of this building, the location of which is significant in that it faces Gaudí's Sagrada Família temple, the city authorities considered it necessary to modify the facade in terms of the vertical series of glazed balconies typical of the Ensanche chamfered corner. The architect commissioned to design the exteriors opted to incorporate a horizontal component, without overlooking the glazed balconies, which are thus linked together by steel-like vertical strips created by the dynamic movement of the balconies.

Other apartment buildings designed by Joan Pascual include those at c/ Rosselló, 395, on the corner of c/ Sicília, 273; at c/ Sant Antoni Maria Claret, 158, and at c/ Rocafort, 80-84, all constructed between 1987 and 1990.

113
Facades of the Hotel Hilton   **1986-1990**

Avenida de la Diagonal, 589
Helio Piñón Pallarés and Albert Viaplana Vea, architects
Bus 6, 7, 33, 34, 66. Metro L3 (Maria Cristina)

The Hilton hotel is another example of the dichotomous architecture referred to above as a recurring feature of the Barcelona of the late eighties. The building was designed by the architects Jordi Mir Valls, Rafael Coll Pujol and Claudi Carmona Sanz, who followed an architectural model then frequently adopted, in accordance with city planning regulations, along that stretch of the Diagonal: free-standing cuboid volumes with sheer facades, generally glazed, with their major axis perpendicular to the Diagonal avenue.

In order to give particular significance to the hotel building, Piñón and Viaplana resorted to a type and tonality of cladding unusual in this setting, together with an accentuation of the habitual proportion of the windows, the sinking of the central plane of the lower part of the facades to emphasize a pi-llar positioned on the axis of the composition, and the siting in front of the main entrance of a singularly tall canopy, this last element being a motif previously utilized by these architects in the plaza dels Països Catalans and subsequently in the Centro de Arte Santa Mònica.

Casa Pedreño

1987-1989

C/ Alberes, 60 (Vallvidrera)
Ramon Artigues Codó and Ramon Sanabria Boix, architects
FF.CC. Generalitat (Peu del Funicular). Funicular de Vallvidrera

The steeply sloping site and the magnificent views over the city determined the general discursive line of this project, oriented on the one hand towards ensuring the effective presence of the new building in its urban and woodland setting, and on the other to providing an effective response to the specific brief for a one-family private residence. The result is a stepped sequence of volumes that adapt to the topography and open up on the basis of their orientation. On the ground floor are the living room and the kitchen, with the bedrooms and games room on the intermediate level and the garage, hall and a study with terrace on the top level. The exterior is of exposed brickwork, wood and glass.

Other noteworthy examples of domestic architecture from this period are the Casa Nassia (c/ Cavallers, 40-42; 1987-1989), designed by the architect Antoni Sunyer Vives, and the Casa Gay (c/ Alberes, 48, in Vallvidrera), by Antoni Moragas Spa and Irene Sánchez Hernando, from 1985-1987.

115
Buildings B1 and B2 of the Escuela de Ingenieros de Caminos, Canales y Puertos 1987-1990

North Campus of the Universitat Politècnica de Catalunya
C/ Gran Capità, 1; c/ Sor Eulàlia de Anzizu, (unnumbered)
Josep Antoni Llinàs Carmona, architect
Bus 7, 75. Metro L3 (Zona Universitària)

Standing opposite one another, their entrances facing, on the longitudinal axis of the campus, the two constructions thus create a small square. Building B1 contains the classrooms, laboratory and services, laid out over a semi-basement and three upper floors, with a raised volume on the western edge. On the facades, the top two floors have continuous strips of windows which are carried around the corners. The main access is sheltered by a canopy which continues along the north facade in the manner of a cornice.

B2 is a cube of the same height as B1. It houses the cafeteria and, on the two upper floors, the lecture hall and the library, lit by zigzagging skylights. These two floors can also be reached by a metal stairway-terrace set against the main facade. A glazed balcony with a trapezoidal plan projects out from the blind wall at first-floor level to let light into the lecture hall. The facades of both buildings are of exposed brickwork with detailing in white aluminium.

Llinàs also designed a CAP public health centre in Cerdanyola del Vallès, at the junction of the main Sabadell-Barcelona road and c/ Tarragona (leading to Ripollet), constructed between 1982 and 1985. Another contemporary public facility is the Bacteriology Service building in the Vall d'Hebron "health-care city" hospital complex in Barcelona, designed by the architect Josep Lluís Canosa Magret (1987).

Building B2.

Building B1.

116
Palacio de la Música Catalana   **1982-1990**

C/ Sant Francesc de Paula, (unnumbered)
Òscar Tusquets Guillén and Carles Díaz Gómez, architects
Bus 16, 17, 19, 45. Metro L1, L2, L4 (Urquinaona)

The intervention in this *Modernista* building by Lluís Domènech Montaner (1905-1908) was based on a sketch design produced by Lluís Clotet and Oscar Tusquets in 1982, which attempted to demonstrate the possibility of a solution to all of the concert hall's problems (of security, acoustics and comfort for audiences and artists), with an effective remodelling of the building making the construction of a new auditorium for the city unnecessary.

The final construction project set out from these premises and the resolve to ensure that the use of the Palacio for symphonic music would be combined with the exercise of its original function as an auditorium for choral music, this proving in effect to be difficult to achieve. The intelligent remodelling and fitting out of the building, and the construction of a new annex, of debatable morphology, resolved the basic problems, although not all of the objectives were fully satisfied. The operation made it necessary to reduce the nave of the neighbouring church of Sant Francesc to accommodate the accesses to the auditorium and the new annex building.

Other contemporary transformations of listed buildings in the city were carried out in the convent of Els Àngels (plaza dels Àngels, unnumbered; 1984-1990; Lluís Clotet Ballús, Ignacio Paricio Ansuategui and Carles Díaz Gómez), remodelled and extended to house the library of Catalonia's art museums, and the Casa Golferichs (Gran Via de les Corts Catalanes, 491; 1987-1988; Joan Ravetllat Mira and Carme Ribas Seix), converted to become a local community centre.

117
Fundación Antoni Tàpies

1986-1990

C/ Aragó, 255
Roser Amadó Cercós and Lluís Domènech Girbau, architects
Bus 7, 16, 17, 22, 24, 28, 43, 544. Metro L3, L5 (Passeig de Gràcia)

The Editorial Montaner i Simon publishing house, an emblematic example of Catalan *Modernista* architecture, was designed by Domènech Montaner in 1879. The standard building height subsequently applied in the Ensanche resulted in the neighbouring constructions dwarfing the lower fabric of the publishing house with their side walls, creating an evident discontinuity in the city block. The new intervention was obliged to resolve this problem without altering the morphology of the building. The solution arrived at by the architects involved the siting on the roof of a projecting structure perpendicular to the facade which would screen off the views of the neighbouring party walls without changing the frontal aspect of the Domènech building. Antoni Tàpies then used this structure as a support for his sculpture "Núvol i cadira" (Chair and cloud), which strikingly identifies the remodelled building.

The richness of this solution and the intelligent remodelling of the interior are in marked contrast to the deterioration of the barely restored facade, typical of the eighties approach to intervention in a monumental building, based on introducing new elements and exploiting the spatial resources and values of the existing building while largely neglecting its material and formal qualities.

The contemporary intervention in the Torre d'Altures or Casa de les Aigües –a neo-Arabic building from 1890– at Ronda del Guinardó, 49, converted to house the municipal offices of the Horta-Guinardó district (Victor Argentí Salvadó, architect; 1985-1989) also lays the emphasis on maintaining the spatial values of the original building.

Polideportivo Palestra
sports centre

1987-1990

Parque de Can Dragó

C/ Rosselló Porcel, (unnumbered); av. de la Meridiana, 425

Miquel Espinet Mestre and Antoni Ubach Nuet, architects

Bus 62, 73, 102, 302. Metro L1 (Fabra i Puig)

The construction of top-level sports facilities for the 1992 Olympic Games did not prevent the implementation of a programme for the construction of much-needed district sports centres around the city. The Palestra sports centre, on a site formerly occupied by the old Sant Andreu railway station –within the new Can Dragó park– was designed primarily as a gymnastics facility.

The two symmetrical wings of the new centre –one for each major branch of gymnastics– have roofs with a structure of large trusses. A central volume containing the entrance vestibule and communal services articulates the two wings, and rises up between them to characterize the unusual appearance of the new facility. The auxiliary rooms are grouped in the lower volumes on the north and south sides of the main central construction, opening to the exterior by way of a series of arches.

The Polideportivo Perill (c/ Perill, 22, by Jaume Bach and Gabriel Mora, 1987) and the Polideportivos Virrei Amat (c/ Joan Alcover, unnumbered, by Manuel Brullet Tenas, 1984-1987) are other interesting sports centres from the same period.

119
Facade of the Hotel Claris

1991

C/ Pau Claris, 150; c/ València, 270
Oriol Bohigas, Josep Martorell, David Mackay and
Albert Puigdomènech, architects
Bus 7, 22, 24, 28, 39, 45, 47. Metro L3, L4 (Passeig de Gràcia)

The celebration of the Olympic Games made it necessary to bring the city's hotel infrastructure up to date, correcting the deficit in quantity and quality. In the Ensanche a considerable number of existing buildings were converted to hotel use, some of them listed buildings of architectural and historical interest. However, even in these cases, the typical approach was to conserve only the facade and replace the interior volume with a new and more cost-effective fabric. In certain instances this practice resulted in an inevitable dichotomy, with different architects being commissioned to design the different parts of the hotel.

This was the case with the Hotel Claris, which took the facade of the Palau Vedruna (constructed in 1892 on a chamfered corner of the Ensanche without occupying the whole of the site) as the publicity "sticker" signposting the new hotel. The side elevations not occupied by the original construction, and the taller volume that rises up to the maximum permitted building height were enclosed within a new curtain-wall.

A similar exercise, perhaps resolved to greater effect, is the extension to the Casa Daurella (paseo de Gràcia, 73) to become the Hotel Comtes de Barcelona (by the architects Josep Juanpere, Antoni Puig and Jordi Romeu; 1991-1992). Other hotel projects from 1991 include the Hotel St. Moritz (c/. Diputació, 262-264; Miquel Espinet, Antoni Ubach); the Gran Hotel Havana (Gran Via de les Corts Catalanes, 647; Josep Juanpere, Antoni Puig) and the Hotel Podium (c/. Bailén, 4; Miquel Bayarri, Josep Gómez, J. Antonio Cordón and Antoni Canal).

120
Núñez Mallorca-Calàbria-Rocafort buildings

1990-1991

C/ Mallorca, 41-43 and 51-53; Calàbria, 191; Rocafort, 174
Carles Ferrater Lambarri, architect
Bus 41, 43, 544. Metro L5 (Entença)

In the course of more than thirty years activity in the Ensanche, the Núñez y Navarro construction company has syccessively modernized its programmes, materials and designs to meet the demands of the market and the city's planning authorities. In the sixties, the firm made repeated use of the building type designed by Enric Rovira Beleta (c/ Calàbria, 162-164, dating from 1959-1960), modelled, at Josep Lluís Núñez's suggestion, on the Marc-Jorba building at Gran Via, 488, by A. Rocabruna (1955), which became the model for a series of buildings dotted across the Ensanche, particularly on its chamfered corners.

In the seventies this model was modified (with the incorporation of large terraces, travertine cladding, etc.) These buildings, by the architect Joan Margarit Serradell, include the Núñez-Trinxet, at c/ Còrsega, 268, 1971-1973 (on the site occupied by the Casa Trinxet); the Núñez-Urgel, at c/ Comte d'Urgell, 224-232, 1971-1974; the Núñez-Liceo (c/ Provença, 325, 1974-1977), on the site of the old Institut Français, an eclectic work from 1900, and so on. Also from this period is the remarkable building at plaza Letamen-

di, 15 (Jordi Vila Robert and Santiago Casanova Navarro, 1977-1980).

In the mid-eighties, social and cultural developments prompted Núñez to engage architects of recognized standing: Carles Ferrater came up with a new model, an updated version of the traditional chamfered corner, used in the building in c/ Mallorca. This period also saw the start of relations with Tusquets, Díaz & Associats, the first fruit of which is the Núñez-Triomf building at paseo Lluís Companys, 23 (1992-1993).

Núñez Mallorca-Calàbria-Rocafort building.

Núñez-Urgel building.

Núñez-Triomf building.

121
Jardins de Can Torras blocks　　　1990-1992

C/ Ramon Turró, 69-109; c/ Llull, 88-102; c/ Zamora, 48; c/ Ávila, 59
Carles Ferrater Lambarri,
with Josep M. Montaner Martorell, architects
Bus 6, 36, 71. Metro L4 (Llacuna)

The maritime sector of the former municipality of Sant Martí de Provençals, long since absorbed into north-eastern Barcelona, is the area of the city most intensely affected by the urban transformations occasioned by the coming of the Olympic Games in 1992. Even before its incorporation into the city in the late 19th century, Sant Martí was an important industrial centre, and continued to be so through to the last quarter of the 20th century. Nowadays the factories have almost all disappeared from the seafront sector, demolished to make way for residences for the Olympic athletes. This conversion of the urban fabric was essentially a public-sector initiative, with the involvement of private capital.

The three blocks of the "Jardins de Can Torras" residential complex –a private development bordering on the Vila Olímpica– stand on the former site of the Torras, Herrerías y Construcciones works which once produced metal girders and pillars used in the construction of the most significant buildings of 19th-century Barcelona. The design of the complex set out from the idea of recreating the typological model of the Cerdà Ensanche block, with a perimeter of residential buildings and leaving the coutyard in the middle of the block free for semi-public recreational uses and other amenities, articulated in the manner of an interior promenade. The passageways at the sides of the corner towers lend emphasis to the austere volmetry, which finds its counterpoint in the treatment of the roofs.

122
Restoration of the Palacio Güell   1989-1992

C/ Nou de la Rambla, 3-5
Antoni González Moreno-Navarro and
Pablo Carbó Berthold, architects
Bus 14, 18, 38, 59, 91. Metro L3 (Liceu, Drassanes)

This building by Antoni Gaudí (1886-1890) was declared a World Heritage monument by the UNESCO in 1985. The restoration scheme was based on the recommendation of the Venice Charter that such monuments be conserved for future generations "with all the richness of their authenticity", but without necessarily confusing this concept with that of originality. Accordingly, in some cases elements in a degraded state were refurbished after rigorous research into their original characteristics, while in others more creative solutions were adopted, in harmonious dialogue with the original fabric. This latter approach was applied to the flat roof, in particular to the replacement of the claddings of the chimneys, which had been lost. The new claddings were designed by the ceramicist Joan Gardy Artigas (chim-ney no. 1), the sculptor Joan Mora (4), the painters Gustavo Carbó Berthold (10) and Robert Llimós (2), and the architects Domingo García Pozuelo, Antoni González (6) and Pablo Carbó (5).

The Casa Milà and Park Güell, other works by Gaudí also declared World Heritage sites by the UNESCO, were also restored at this time, the Casa Milà –La Pedrera– by the architects Josep Emili Hernández Cros and Rafael Vila Rodríguez (1987-1991), and the park by J. A. Martínez Lapeña and Elías Torres Tur (1986-1990). These latter architects carried out an imaginative intervention (1986-1990) on the roofs of the Palau de les Heures, by August Font Carreras (1894-1895), next to the Hogares Mundet, restored by Pablo Carbó in 1990 and now occupied by one of the city's universities.

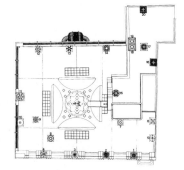

123
Pavilion of the Spanish Republic (reconstruction)

1992

C/ Jorge Manrique, (unnumbered);
Av. Cardenal Vidal i Barraquer, (unnumbered)
Miquel Espinet Mestre, Antoni Ubach Nuet and
José Miguel Hernández León, architects
Bus 27, 45, 73, 76, 85. Metro L3 (Montbau)

The decision to reconstruct the pavilion designed by Josep Lluís Sert (in collaboration with Luis Lacasa) to represent the Spanish Republic at the 1937 Paris Exhibition emerged from a concern with recapturing outstanding instances of the architecture of the Modern Movement, although –unlike the Mies van der Rohe pavilion– Sert's pavilion had no direct relationship with Barcelona. The euphoria with which the city set about regenerating its urban fabric during its Olympiad greatly aided the initiative. In due course, King Juan Carlos formally opened the reconstruction of the Republican pavilion.

The reconstruction scheme required in-depth study of the long-demolished original, little precise information about which had survived. The construction project thus took into consideration the character and use of the original pavilion, conceived as a showroom structured along the one-way itinerary which directed visitors through the building; the only modifications were those required by current standards of safety, architectural barriers, etc. This is the case with the basement, which contains the services, and the addition of a new block of offices to the pavilion. The materials and colours used in the reconstruction are as faithful as possible to those employed by Sert in the original.

In front of the pavilion is the sculpture *Mistos* (Matches) by Claes Oldenburg and Coosje van Bruggen.

124
Els Balcons de Barcelona
gap-site facade

1992

Plaza de la Hispanitat, (unnumbered); c/ Enamorats, 5
Cité de la Création
Bus 18, 35, 56, 62

In 1986, with the slogan "Barcelona, posa't guapa" (Barcelona, make yourself pretty), the city council launched a campaign to encourage the cleaning up and restoration of facades and the upgrading of all those elements seen as defining the urban landscape. Despite the setting up of a technical advisory office to support the initiative, questions of commercial and political advantage ultimately prevailed and the quality of the results was sacrificed in favour of quantity and publicity. There were only a few genuine restorations, two of which were directed by the architect Rafael Vila Rodríguez: the facades of the Casa Amatller (paseo de Gràcia, 41; 1989) and of the Casa Piña, "El Regulador" (Rambla, 105; 1990).

One of the objectives of the campaign was to intervene in the appearance of gap-site walls where the location and the absence of plans for future construction made these a permanent element in the urban landscape. The wall overlooking the plaza de la Hispanitat was treated in the manner of a pictorial mural reproducing an Ensanche facade, on the balconies of which stand twenty-one men and women associated with the city in different historical periods: Christopher Columbus, Raquel Meller, Pablo Picasso, Antoni Gaudí, Francesc Macià, Jacint Verdaguer, Carmen Amaya, Joan Miró, Pau Casals, etc. Other gap-site walls similarly treated as facades were those at General Mitre, 54 (Pepita Teixidor, architect, 1987), and those at Gran de Gràcia, 262-264, and Ronda de la Universitat, 1 (both by Joan Manuel Nicolàs, 1990-1991).

125
Teixonera senior citizens' residence and day centre

1988-1992

c/ Josep Sangenís, (unnumbered); plaza de la Clota
Josep Emili Donato Folch, architect

Bus 19, 86

The building rises up in the form of a monumental screen-cum-pergola separating a densely built sector –on the edge of the Carmel district– from an appreciably lower sector containing the Area de la Vall d'Hebron Olympic installations, with extensive landscaped spaces. The plan is developed as a semi-circle, constituting a paved plaza which closes in on itself and provides access to the apartments as well as an area for recreation and contact.

The building is organized as two clearly differentiated zones: in one sector are the apartments, radially ordered, with a central corridor, while the other half is left as an empty pergola, interrupted by a solid cylindrical volume, a rotunda occupied by communal spaces and services. The unifying element in the complex is marked by the line of the roof, which is also differentiated in its two stretches. The construction is austere in its use of forms and materials –exposed brickwork and plain tile cladding– with an interesting play of solids and voids, a characteristic feature of Emili Donato's architecture.

The same architect also designed the contemporaneous Sant Ildefons public health centre in Av. República Argentina in Cornella de Llobregat (1989-1991).

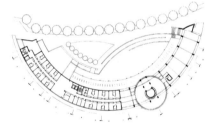

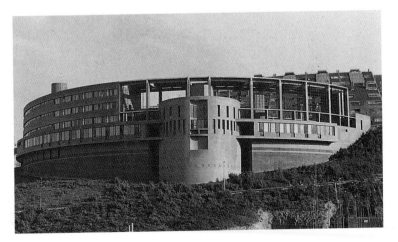

Hotel Juan Carlos I

1988-1992

Avenida de la Diagonal, 661-671
Carles Ferrater Lambarri and
Josep M. Cartañà Gubern, architects
Bus 7, 75. Metro L3 (Zona Universitària)

The hotel was constructed on the site of the old "Torre Melina", a 17th-century farmhouse which, despite its historical and architectural significance, and the protests of local people, was demolished by the developers, who then decided to change the name of the hotel, which was originally to have referred to the old house.

The design of the new building embodies a complex range of services structured in four zones: a fitness centre; a leisure centre with a functions room with capacity for a thousand guests; a sector with an auditorium, a convention hall, a business centre, an underground car park, and the hotel itself, and an exterior plaza in front of the main entrance.

Two large screen-like walls of concrete, trapezoidal in plan, containing ducting and vertical services, flank the entrance. Behind these are two wings set at an obtuse angle which compose the great full-height vestibule or interior plaza –separated from the exterior plaza by a great glass wall– overlooked by the corridors leading to the bedrooms, and dominated by the shafts of the panoramic lifts. The general organization of the hotel, together with the decoration scheme, follow the style characteristic of hotels in North America. During the 1992 Olympic Games, the hotel was the headquarters of the various organizing committees.

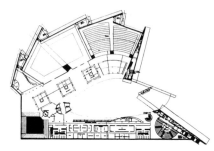

127
Collserola Telecommunications Tower

1989-1992

Turó de Vilana. Tibidabo
Norman Foster & Partners, architects
Funicular del Tibidabo (Peu del Funicular)

The tower is, alongside the Sant Jordi sports pavilion, the most emblematic element constructed for the 1992 Olympics. Its situation, on one of the peaks of the Collserola range of hills, making it visible from a large part of the Barcelona area, and its remarkable architectural form, contribute to making it a monumental landmark overlooking the urban landscape of the city.

The construction of the tower was motivated by the need to reorganize the various communications installations scattered over the Collserola hills and other parts of the city and improve the efficacy of the existing systems. The structure of the tower consists of a cylindrical concrete inner core 205.5 metres high; a great metallic structure with a curving triangular plan accommodating thirteen platforms or levels, measuring 75 metres from top to bottom; three sets of pre-tensed metal cables anchored to the lowest of these platforms; three fibre ties connecting the crown of the metal structure to the concrete shaft, and an 85-metre metal

mast rising up from the top of the core. One of the upper platforms serves as a public observation balcony, with its own access independent of the technical installations.

Norman Foster described the tower as "pure sculpture... the smallest needle on the sensible line of the horizon".

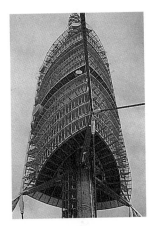

Montjuïc Olympic Ring

1985-1992

Av. de l'Estadi; paseo de Minici Natal
Carles Buxadé, Federico Correa,
Joan Margarit and Alfonso Milá, architects
Bus 13, 61. Metro L1, L3 (Espanya, Paral.lel). Funicular de Montjuïc

The laying out and urbanization of the Olympic Ring on Montjuïc was the result of an international limited competition organized by the Ayuntamiento de Barcelona in 1983. The winning project was felt to have successfully handled issues such as the relationship with the surrounding landscape, the clarity of the ordering of the series of elements, the perception of the buildings and their symbolic value and the inter-relating of the various facilities.

The complex as a whole is structured on the basis of an axis adapted to the topography of the hill as it drops down from the Olympic Stadium to the INEFC national physical education institute and configures a series of terraces or plazas bordered by the other facilities, such as the Palacio Sant Jordi sports pavilion, the Bernat Picornell swimming pools and the telecommunications tower. The different levels are connected by flights of steps, water courses and cascades, and paved or grass-covered esplanades, all presided over by the lighting pillars that flank the main axis and culminate in a circular plaza –the plaza de Europa– laid out on top of a 60,000 m^3 water tank.

The INEFC building (1988-1991) was designed by the architect Ricardo Bofill Levi. With capacity for 1000 students and a staff of 100 teachers, it is constructed of architectural concrete, using prefabricated and in situ elements. Classical in appearance, the building is organized around two great

The INEFC building.

The Olympic Ring. In the foreground, the telecommunications tower.

roofed cloisters linked by a central hall which contains the vestibule and the functions and exhibition suite.

The Picornell swimming pools, constructed for the 1970 European swimming championships, were skilfully remodelled by the architects Franc Fernández and Moisés Gallego during 1990 and 1991. The complex has two open-air pools, of 25 by 50 and 25 by 25 metres, and a 25 by 50 metres indoor pool.

The telecommunications tower, not included in the original scheme, was designed by Santiago Calatrava and built in 1991 on the east side of the second plaza. It is conceived as a sculpture on the urban scale, 120 metres in height, visible from much of the metropolitan area. Constructed of white-painted steel, the mast is inclined at the same angle as the Earth's axis, and thus functions as a sun dial. The form of the base and the trencadis ceramic cladding are a homage to Antoni Gaudí.

The old Montjuïc municipal swimming pool, built in 1929 on the Av. de Miramar, some 600 m from the Stadium, was refurbished –by Antoni de Moragas Spa (1991-1992)– to accommodate the Olympic water polo and diving competitions.

Picornell swimming pools. Indoor pool.

Picornell swimming pools. Exterior facade.

Montjuïc Olympic Stadium

1986-1990

Av. de l'Estadi; paseo de Minici Natal
Vittorio Gregotti with Carles Buxadé, Federico Correa,
Joan Margarit and Alfonso Milá, architects
Bus 13, 61. Metro L1, L3 (Espanya, Paral.lel). Funicular de Montjuïc

The old Montjuïc Stadium, constructed for Barcelona's International Exhibition in 1929, was for long the physical symbol of the city's Olympic aspirations. In spite of its poor state of conservation, the decision to adapt it to become the principal scenario for the 1992 Games can be seen, in the words of the critic Lluís de Grassot, as reflecting the city's resolve "not to renounce the past at the moment of planning the future".

The remodelling was entrusted to Vittorio Gregotti, who had submitted a scheme for the international competition organized by the Ayuntamiento de Barcelona in collaboration with Correa, Milá, Margarit and Buxadé. Richard Weidler joined the team as technical supervisor and consultant in sports architecture.

The level of the playing field and track was lowered by eleven metres –a difficult operation in view of the rocky terrain– in order to increase the capacity of the stand, which was entirely reconstructed to accommodate almost 60,000 seated spectators. The original facade of the Stadium was restored, providing the monumental backdrop to the longitudinal axis of the Ring, and

the gateway for the Marathon, although it is no longer used as the finish for that gruelling event. A metal canopy 150 m long with a projection of 30 m was installed, perhaps the most unsuccessful element of the new intervention. At the same time, the sculptures *Charioteers* and *Riders giving the Olympic salute*, produced by Pau Gargallo for the 1929 stadium, were restored and replaced in their original position.

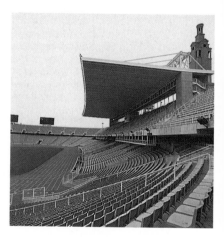

130
Palacio de Deportes Sant Jordi   1985-1990

Av. de l'Estadi; paseo de Minici Natal
Arata Isozaki & Associates
Bus 13, 61. Metro L1, L3 (Espanya, Paral.lel). Funicular de Montjuïc

The Palacio Sant Jordi in Barcelona, together with the Palacio Municipal d'Esports in Badalona (Av. Alfons XII - c/ Ponent) by Esteve Bonell Costa and Francesc Rius Camps (1989-1990), are the two buildings constructed for the 1992 Summer Olympic Games most praised by the international critics. The first has rapidly attained the status of architectonic emblem of Barcelona, alongside the city's most significant historical monuments.

The sports pavilion is actually composed of two buildings: the main Palacio Principal, seating 17,000 spectators; and the Pavellón Polivalente, rectangular in plan and covered by a flat metal roof. The roof of the Palacio Principal, a space frame which constitutes one of the most provocative spaces in the city's architecture, was assembled on the ground and raised into position by means of a sophisticated system of hydraulic jacks. This structure is surrounded by a portico adapted to the topography, its undulating roof giving lightness and dynamism to the whole.

In the main access plaza in front of the pavilion is the sculpture *Change,* a series of concrete pillars sprouting stainless steel wands, by the Japanese artist Aiko Miyawaki. In the main vestibules of the Palacio Sant Jordi are two murals by the painter J. Hernández Pijoan, entitled *Flors per als campions* (Flowers for the champions), and two by A. Ràfols Casamada, entitled *Mar* (Sea) and *Terra* (Land).

Mar Bella sports pavilion

1989-1992

Cinturó del Litoral. Mar Bella beach. Parc de Poblenou
Manuel Ruisánchez Capelastegui and Xavier Vendrell Sala, architects
Bus 6, 36, 92. Metro L4 (Llacuna, Poblenou)

The Parque del Poblenou, the athletics track and the Pavellón de la Mar Bella are three physically contiguous interventions by the same team of architects, all forming part of the complex of public spaces and amenities that is Barcelona's new seafront. The project for the park was conceived as a landscape of dunes and pine trees, with pedestrian itineraries connecting the rectilinear streets perpendicular to the sea which are themselves crossed by curving paths parallel to the coastline.

The Pavellón de la Mar Bella appears in this landscaped setting as an uncompromisingly geometrical figure, standing on the north-eastern edge of the park; one of the most beautiful constructions created for the 1992 Olympic Games.

The building consists of a main volume, housing the multi-sports hall and the spectator seating, and a partially sunken perimetral base on top of which is a cultural centre with a library, housing the services. The structure of the pavilion is composed of a series of diaphragms spanning fifty metres, formed by metal beams and concrete screens, with an inverted roof. The skin between the screens is of sheets of plate glass in the interior, the lower part transitable, and perforated metal panels on the exterior. The side facades have panels of laminated wood suspended over a glazed horizontal strip.

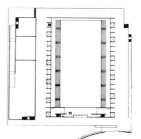

132
Vall d'Hebron Olympic Area   **1989-1991**

Paseo de la Vall d'Hebron; parque de la Clota
Eduard Bru Bistuer, architect (general urban design scheme)
Bus 27, 45, 73, 76, 85. Metro L3 (Montbau)

This, one of the four 1992 Olympic areas, is on the north side of the city, on the lower slopes of the Collserola range. The location, with its abrupt changes in level, conditioned the laying out of this sector on the basis of platforms looking out over the city. The urban design project by Eduard Bru is articulated in four major zones: the cycle track, above the Ronda de Dalt, and below this the sports zone (including the Pavellón de la Vall d'Hebron, the archery fields, the Centro Municipal de Tenis, a swimming-pool complex and multi-sports track above the Sant Genis bus depot), the residential (the Press Village during the 1992 Olympics) and hotel zone, and, in the lowest sector, the Clota park with the reconstructed Pavilion of the Spanish Republic and a series of monumental sculptures.

The urbanization of this whole area is approached on the basis of a series of elements (roads, footpaths, footbridges, steps, banks and terraces, gardens, architectonic and sculptural objects, street furniture and lighting), the ordering and form of which reflect a concern with innovation and experimentation in design and materials, taking advantage of the historic opportunity provided by the Olympic Games. The use of synthetic materials in outdoor pavings, the metal kerbing of the footpaths, the signage and the trees, arranged in an unusual and effective layout, the monumental itineraries, the railings, the pergolas, are all interesting contributions to contemporary urban design.

Pergolas and sports pavilion in the background.

Sports pavilion.

Of the new buildings, the most significant is the Pavellón de la Vall d'Hebron, by the architects Jordi Garcés and Enric Sòria, from 1990-1991. This contains two independent sports facilities: the Centre Municipal de Pilota and the Palacio Municipal de Deporte. The complex is resolved in the form of a great cuboid with an almost flat metal roof, from which the linear skylights project. The facades, of exposed brickwork, are sheer, and clearly reveal the interior organization of the building (accesses, emergency exits, changing rooms, services, etc.). This approach gives the building an abstract, minimalist quality in the complex context in which it stands.

The Camp de Tir amb Arc –the archery field (1990-1991)– in c/ Basses d'Horta and Martí Codolar includes a training and warm-up area and the competition field, separated by a new road. The large level expanses of grass these facilities require justify the treatment of the buildings as containing walls which penetrate the terrain with their prefabricated concrete elements and metal pergolas, intentionally laid out in a disordered arrangement to create a variety of planes and axes that is a characteristic of the work of the architects, Enric Miralles and Carme Pinós.

The Centro Municipal de Tenis "Vall d'Hebron" (designed by Antoni Sunyer Vives, 1990-1991) is situated in c/ Pare Clariana. The sries of seventeen courts is adapted to the sloping terrain as a sequence of platforms separated by transverse concrete walls which extend out to the exterior of the

Archery fields.

Archery fields.

club precincts to constitute a kind of monumental wedge. At the highest point of the complex is a triangular plaza, beneath which are the services.

The "Nou Vall d'Hebron" residential development (used as the Press Village during the Olympic Games) is laid out around the plaza Joan Cornudella, with access from c/ Berruguete. It was designed by Carles Ferrater, Josep M. Cartañá, Joan Josep Forcadell, Ferran Pla and Robert Suso. Two high-rise apartment blocks preside over the entrance to the square, which is bounded laterally by two screen blocks and at the back by a sinuous, stepped, linear building that follows the line of the road –the Torrent dels Garrofers de Can Travi– and closes off the eastern boundary of the Olympic Area. The treatment of the facades with panels of white artifi-

cial stone, and the pronounced horizontal of the openings, clearly distinguish the complex out from the surrounding urban fabric.

Longitudinal section of the Pavellón de la Vall d'Hebron, J. Garcés and E. Sòria, architects.

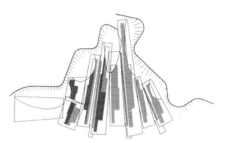

Plan of the Camp de Tir amb Arc training and warm-up building.

The Olympic Village

1985-1992

C/ de la Marina; c/ Moscou; c/ Doctor Trueta; av. Bogatell;
c/ Bisbe Climent; ronda del Litoral.
Oriol Bohigas, Josep Martorell, David Mackay and Albert Puigdomènech,
architects (general urban design and parks)
Bus 6, 36, 71, 92. Metro L4 (Ciutadella, Bogatell)

The Olympic Village (also known as Nova Icària in memory of the 19th-century Utopian socialists who founded a settlement in the area) extends over a zone of more than 150 hectares along the coastline, formerly occupied by old and for the most part obsolete industrial buildings which, together with the railway tracks, constituted a barrier between the city and the sea. The need to construct the Olympic athletes' residences set in motion one of the greatest urban operations of late 20th-century Barcelona.

Almost 2,000 apartments were built, as well as two 44-storey tower blocks– one for offices, the other a hotel –and a sports port and other facilities related to the sea, one-off office buildings and a group of new services attached to the city's Hospital del Mar. The new Villa Olímpica was also provided with its own sports centre and a parish church, which served as an ecumenical centre during the Games. In addition, the operation involved the remodelling of the main railway and road systems, the restructuring of the Bogatell surface water drainage outfall, the creation of 50 hectares of parks and the reclaiming of the beaches, opening the city to the sea once again.

The residential area is laid out on the basis of semi-open blocks following the regular grid of the Cerdà Ensanche; the interiors of these accommodate gardens, amenities of various kinds and in a few cases back-to-back terraced houses. The design of each of the residential buildings was entrusted to

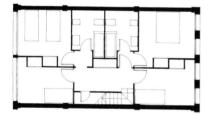

"Xemeneia de Can Folch". Apartment, lower floor.

"Xemeneia de Can Folch". Apartment, upper floor.

"Xemeneia de Can Folch" block (c/ Moscou). MBM and Puigdomènech, architects.

Buildings in c/ Doctor Trueta on the corner of c/. Arquitecte Sert. Ricardo Bofill, architect.

one of the architects or teams of architects who had won a FAD Arquitectura prize, awarded annually since 1958. The final result reveals a great disparity of formal approaches (in some ways comparable to what happened in Berlin with the IBA between 1982 and 1987), a low level of construction quality, and a level of creativity that is in no case equal to that demonstrated by the architects concerned in their earlier work.

Amongst the residential buildings are: the "Xemeneia de Can Folch" block (c/ Moscou, c/ de la Marina), by the team of Martorell-Bohigas-Mackay and Puigdomènech, which follows the curving line of the railway, rerouted underground, and conserves the chimney of the old Folch factory; the block designed by the Correa-Milá studio, in c/ Salvador Espriu, between carrer de la Marina and c/ Joan Miró, which recovers the balconies and glazed galleries of the Ensanche; the buildings facing onto the seafront by Esteve Bonell, Francesc Rius and J. M. Gil, in c/ Salvador Espriu, between c/ Arquitecte Sert and c/ Frederic Mompou, with an interesting "triplex" solution of the layout; the buildings designed by Ricardo Bofill, in c/ Doctor Trueta on the corner of c/ Arquitecte Sert, and the plaza Tirant lo Blanc complex, by J. A. Martínez Lapeña and E. Torres Tur, developed on the basis of an open circular plan, with a tower block presiding over one side (awarded the Fad de Arquitectura prize 1992).

There are a number of service buildings along the seafront: the Mapfre Tower, by Iñigo Ortiz and Enrique León, and the Hotel de les Arts with its

The plaza Tirant lo Blanc complex. Typical apartment.

The plaza Tirant lo Blanc complex. J. A. Martínez Lapeña and E. Torres Tur, architects.

various annexes, by Bruce Graham (of Skidmore, Owings & Merrill) and Frank O. Gehry, these two high-rise blocks being the same in volumetry and height but very different in formal treatment; and the Meteorological Service and Coastal Demarcation building, by the architect Alvaro Siza Vieira, in the form of a hermetic cylinder of white marble resting on a concrete base, with a hollow cylindrical core.

The parks that border the Olympic Village on its west, south and east sides are divided into different stretches, designed by a different team of architects: the Parc de Carles I, between two curving boundaries, was laid out by Josep Zazurca; the sequence consisting of the Parque de les Cascades, the Parque del Port and the Parque d'Icària, by the MBM and Puigdomènech team, are developed longitudinally between the Ronda del Litoral and the Paseo Marítim; on the eastern edge is the Parque del Poblenou, designed by Manuel Ruisánchez and Xavier Vendrell. Along the axis of the Av. d'Icària, which is the principal thoroughfare of the Villa Olímpica, terminating at the Cementiri Est cemetery, is a great pergola by Enric Miralles and Carme Pinós; fashioned out of wooden slats on metal uprights, this somehow seems to evoke a longed-for avenue of trees.

The Meteorological Service and Coastal Demarcation building. Alvaro Siza Vieira, architect.

The Mapfre Tower (the nearer of the two) and the Hotel de les Arts.

134
Puerto Olímpico

1989-1992

C/ de la Marina; ronda del Litoral
Oriol Bohigas, Josep Martorell, David Mackay and
Albert Puigdomènech, architects; J. Ramon de Clascà, civil engineer
Bus 36, 41, 71. Metro L4 (Ciutadella-Vila Olímpica)

The port, constructed opposite the Olympic Village, is situated at the end of a monumental north-south promenade that begins at the Fuente Monumental fountain in the plaza dels Voluntaris (by the architect Josep M. Mercé Hospital), continues between the two skyscrapers, and concludes in the car park esplanade, passing on its way the spectacular metal sculpture of a fish by the architect Frank O. Gehry.

The Port is quadrangular in plan, with a great, slightly curving sea wall some 500 metres in length; it has a stepped section, on the upper level of which is the pedestrian promenade leading to the harbour mouth, and the quays on the lower level, accommodating maritime and civic activities. The elevated north-eastern promenade is occupied by four restaurant buildings, a linear pergola with commanding views of the port, and the Escuela Municipal de Vela sailing school. At the western edge of the service quay is the Reception Building. Both of these latter elements were conceived as a modular system of cuboids, and thus evidence a certain compositional unity. The Escuela de Vela sailing school is distinguished by its roofs: the pure white walls of these apparently disorderly truncated quarter pyramids create attractive effects of changing light and shade, and call to mind the sails that symbolize the building's function.

The Escuela de Vela sailing school.

The Villa Olímpica
gateway buildings

1989-1992

Bus 36, 41, 71. Metro L4 (Ciutadella-Vila Olímpica)

Designed to accommodate offices and services, these buildings stand on the major traffic axes of the Olympic Village, between the superbocks of the housing, and in view of their singular character were allowed greater freedom of composition, volume and materials that the residential buildings. It is by way of these gateway buildings that the streets running perpendicular to the shoreline connect the Villa Olímpica with the rest of the Ensanche.

Telefónica telephone exchange
C/ Joan Miró, unnumbered; av. de Icària
Jaume Bach Núñez and Gabriel Mora
Gramunt, architects

This is composed of two volumes linked by a third element raised above the level of the street. The first two, quite different in their volumetries (a prism with a rectangular plan and trapezoidal section, and a cylinder with an elliptical plan), are independent of one another, and house, respectively, the offices and the technical installations of the telephone exchange. The vertical communications cores are on the facing sides of the two volumes, with the duality of their functions reflected on the exterior by the treatment of their facades: the walls of the prism are virtually blind, clad in stone, while the cylinder is finished in corrugated aluminium, with continuous strips of windows under subtle sunshades that project out from the plane of the facade. The bridge volume that connects the two buildings is inclined to adapt to the diffence in level of their vertical communications.

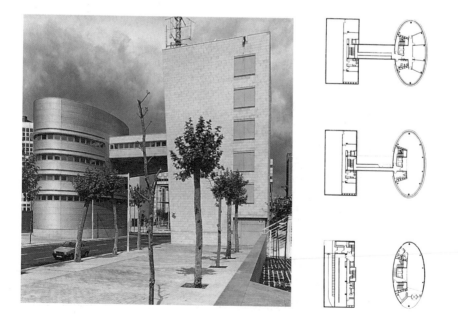

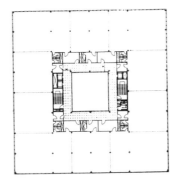

Eurocity 1 office building
C/ Joan Miró, unnumbered;
Av. de Icària
Roser Amadó Cercós and
Lluís Domènech Girbau, architects

"More than a gateway", the architects affirm, "this is a triumphal arch, a defensive bulwark that protects the entrance to the block as the Mediaeval turret did, in the interior of which there was a parade ground that has here become a light well that organizes the distribution of the offices on the two top floors." Although the construction rises to a height of six storeys, only the top two are enclosed in the form of a cubic mass of granite and glass containing the offices, held up by two solid towers housing the vertical communications and the services, and a series of perimetral metal pillars.

The Eurocity 1 office building; in the foreground, the pergolas of the Av. Icària by E. Miralles and C. Pinós, architects.

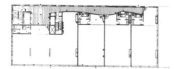

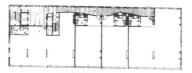

Plantas cuarta y quinta.

Eurocity 2, 3 and 4 office buildings
C/ Rosa Sensat (junction with
Av. d'Icària and c/ Doctor Trueta)
Helio Piñón Pallarés and
Albert Viaplana Vea, architects

The criteria applied to these three "gateways", identical in form and size, were based on the fracturing of the volumetry and the perspective view, the buildings being conceived as cuboids with the interior stepping up to the line of the crown, so that the volume takes on the form of an inverted corbel. The seaward facades are treated as curtain-walls, while the other elevations are clad in marble.

136
Sant Abraham parish church
(Abraham Ecumenical Centre) 1990-1992

C/ Jaume Vicens i Vives, 2; c/ Bisbe Climent
Josep Benedito Rovira and Agustí Mateos Duch, architects
Bus 36, 41, 71. Metro L4 (Ciutadella-Vila Olímpica)

The church stands on the eastern edge of the Olympic Village, by the gates of the old Cementiri Est cemetery, occupying its own small block. The form of the church is established by a series of curving walls that compose an elliptical envelope around the main volume of the temple itself and a second, triangular service volume. In plan, the church has the symbolically significant form of a stylized fish.

During the 1992 Olympic Games the building was the setting for the celebration of services and liturgical acts by the various religious persuasions with significant numbers of adherents amongst the competitors. Since the end of the Olympiad, it has been the Catholic parish church serving the new residential neighbourhood, while retaining its ecumenical vocation.

Other public facilities constructed in the Villa Olímpica include the Pavellón Polideportiu multi-sports centre, situated on a triangular site bounded by Av. d'Icària, c/ del Arquitecte Sert and Av. del Bogatell, designed by the architects Franc Fernández and Moisés Gallego, and the Health Centre (at present the Social Security emergency coordinating centre) at c/ Joan Miró, 17, by the architects Sergi Godia, Josep Urgell and M. Pilar de la Villa.

Multi-sports centre in Av. d'Icària.

New roads and communications infrastructure

The celebration of the Olympic Games provided Barcelona with the opportunity to carry through to completion the road network for the city and the surrounding area envisaged in the urban renewal programme: communications between districts, improved accesses, new ring roads.

The implementation of these operations produced some outstanding civil engineering: the double bridge by the engineers José Antonio Fernández Ordóñez and Julio Martínez Calzón (in collaboration with the architect Lorenzo Fernández Ordóñez) in c/ Sardenya, between Alí-Bey and Almogàvers (1989-1992), and three interventions by the firm of Fernández Casado (engineers Leonardo Fernández Troyano and Javier Manterola) between 1990 and 1992: the traffic interchanges of Collserola, Trinitat and Borràs, on the new ring road (an expressway with a generally high level of formal design). Equally deserving of note are the Les Drassanes rotunda (Av. Paral.lel - Paseo Josep Carner), with its evocative "smoke fountain" (Pedro Barragán, architect, and IMPUSA technical staff), and the new plaza de les Glòries Cata-

lanes (1991-1992) by the architect Andreu Arriola Madorell, both for the park between the pillars of the viaducts as for the viaducts themselves, designed in collaboration with the engineer Adolfo Monclús Jurado.

These new communications routes, and the reform of a number of existing roads, entailed the provision of a series of complementary elements which in some cases were designed with special attention to their integration into the urban landscape. A good example is the design of the footbridges over the Via Favència by the architects Josep Ignasi de Llorens Duran and Alfons Soldevila Barbosa, constructed in 1992: one running parallel to the Av. Meridiana (with a handsome pergola), and the footbridge-bench opposite the Canyelles estate, although not constructed as originally designed. For the junction of Via Favència and Via Júlia, Llorens and Soldevila came up with a remarkable skylight, and a complex pergola for c/ Aragó. These same architects also laid out the public facilities on the covered stretches of the Ronda del Litoral in the Baró de Viver and Bon Pastor districts.

Traffic interchange at plaza Borràs.

The metal footbridge by Carlos Fernández Casado in its new position.

In 1992, the metal footbridge designed by Carlos Fernández Casado in 1972 for the plaza de les Glòries was relocated over the Ronda del Litoral, and adapted to its new position with the addition of concrete ramps designed by the engineers Leonardo Fernández Troyano and Javier Manterola.

Another type of infrastructure that had to be modernized in line with this profound process of urban reform was the underground drainage and sewage system. This produced both negative and positive consequences. Amongst the former is the destruction (in September 1989) of some valuable archaeological remains of the city's 18th-century fortress, unnecessarily demolished in the routing of the new main surface-water drains from the hills to the sea through the Ciutadella park. Amongst the positive consequences is the creation of the educational "García Fària" exhibition centre, under the paseo de Sant Joan just below its meeting with the Av. Diagonal, by the architect Xavier Güell (1991-1992).

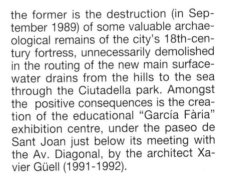

The new plaza de les Glòries Catalanes.

Pedestrian bridge over Via Favència parallel to Avinguda Meridiana.

The "García Fària" exhibition centre in the paseo de Sant Joan.

138
Barcelona Airport Terminal building   1989-1992

El Prat de Llobregat
Ricardo Bofill - Taller de Arquitectura
RENFE railway station (Aeroport) (departures from El Clot,
Arc de Triomf, Plaça de Catalunya and Sants)

Like so many others, Barcelona airport is not situated within the city boundaries, but it may nevertheless be considered as forming part of Barcelona's architectural patrimony. The airport at El Prat was opened in 1949, on the basis of the original Muntadas aerodrome. In 1968 a new terminal was constructed, decorated two years after its inauguration with a ceramic mural designed by Joan Miró and produced by Llorens Artigas. In 1989, with the Olympic Games in mind, it was decided to extend the terminal to provide capacity for up to twelve million passengers a year.

The passenger terminals (the remodelled 1968 building and the two new buildings) are laid out in a line, with an esplanade almost 800 metres long connecting the three at an upper level. This esplanade and the three terminal buildings are unified by the use of the same reddish stone paving throughout, with the various services (restaurants, kiosks, shops, information desks, etc.) occupying free-standing volumes with a skin of glass or white stone. Off the esplanade, three triangular bays projecting out over the apron contain the embarcation lounges, with a total of 24 air-jetty connections for boarding.

The language utilized by Ricardo Bofill combines a perhaps slightly exhausted classicism with moments of technological exhibitionism. The solution of the facades, however, in the form of a double skin of dark glass with transparent bands enveloping the metal load-bearing structure, is highly expressive.

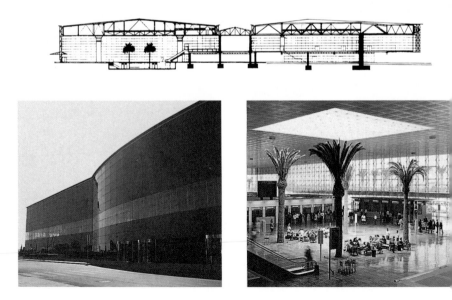

139
Hospital del Mar

1989-1992

Paseo Marítim, 25-29; c/ del Gas
Manuel Brullet Tenas and Albert de Pineda Álvarez, architects
Bus 45, 59. Metro L4 (Ciutadella-Vila Olímpica)

Another building whose remodelling was begun in 1989 with the '92 Olympics in mind is the old Hospital de Infecciosos de Barcelona, designed by the architect Josep Plantada in 1925, which was to be the Olympic Hospital. The original complex consists of seven independent pavilions laid out in parallel and communicating by way of the central transverse axis which opens off the main entrance. Over the years, the complex had undergone various reforms and extensions –in 1973 a tower block was constructed to house the neurology department, with an annexe for surgical operations– which had significantly altered the original unitary structure and volume.

The present remodelling and extension are intended by the architects to satisfy two objectives: on the one hand, the definition of a new organizational, functional and physical structure for the hospital centre, retaining the concept of free-standing pavilions, and on the other, to adapt it to the urban development and planning operations prompted by the construction of the Olympic Village along the neighbouring stretch of seafront. The new model of seafront facade, with a linear development to adapt to the new line of the promenade, the communal access zones such as the slender pallium of the vestibule with their lightweight metal structures that generate diaphanous spaces, the homely atmosphere created by the landscaped areas and the extensive use of daylight, together with the furnishings, all reflect a concern with giving the hospital complex an image more in harmony with the new Olympic buildings nearby.

The urban block occupied by the hospital is completed on the north side with another building –which accommodates the Faculty of Medicine of the Universitat Autònoma de Barcelona and the Institut Municipal d'Investigacions Mèdiques– designed by the architects J. Margarit and C. Buxadé.

Hotel Plaza

1990-1993

Plaza de Espanya, 8
Jordi Garcés Brusés and Enric Sòria Badia, architects
Bus 9, 27, 50, 56, 61, 109. Metro L1, L3 (Espanya)

The new hotel replaces the hotel built for the 1929 International Exhibition by Rubió Tudurí, which was demolished, and its siting on the plaza de Espanya –which still conserves a number of 1929 buildings and the Arenas bullring (whose brickwork facade evokes the texture of the demolished hotel)– produces evident discord. Nor does the new structure readily integrate into the c/. Tarragona, the new tertiary axis running tangentially off the circular plaza with a sequence of four much taller high-rise towers.

The hotel building, pentagonal in plan, is organized around a central courtyard whose walls are clad in ceramic tiles of a washed-out blue inspired by the tiling of the stair well in Gaudí's Casa Batlló. The cladding of the exterior facades is of two tones of granite, grey and red, with a rhythmical geometric pattern of the joints combining regularly with the rhythm of the window openings and the forms of the detail. The large clock on the main facade recalls the clock of Rubió Tudurí's 1929 hotel.

Another new hotel, also constructed with a view to the 1992 Olympics, is the Hotel Citadines (Rambla, 122, 1988-1992) by Esteve Bonell and Josep M. Gil Guitart, who very successfully resolved the problems of building on a narrow gap site next to a monumental neighbour. A little way away from this is the "intelligent" office and car-park building of the Palau Nou de la Rambla (Rambla, 94, 1990-1994), by the MBM team in collaboration with the architects Jordi Frontons, Carles Buxadé and Joan Margarit.

141
Archivo de la Corona de Aragón   1990-1993

Plaza de les Arts; av. de Carles I
Roser Amadó Cercós and Lluís Domènech Girbau, architects
Bus 6, 42, 141. Metro L1 (Marina)

The new building containing the historic Archives of the Crown of Aragon, formerly housed in the Palau del Lloctinent, alongside the cathedral, was constructed on the immense level expanse adjoining the Marina bridge as part of a wide-ranging operation to endow this part of the city with cultural and public amenities and create a new monumental axis that would truly attain that quality of centrality intended for this avenue since Ildefons Cerdà's original plan of 1859. Laid out around the new plaza de les Arts, at the confluence of c/ Marina (known until quite recently as Carlos I) and the Meridiana avenue, are the Estación del Norte public park and the new intercity bus station, the Arxiu, the Teatro Nacional de Catalunya (by the architect Ricardo Bofill), and the new Auditorium, designed by the architect Rafael Moneo Vallés.

The new Archivo de la Corona de Aragón building, a highly distinctive landmark visible from a considerable distance, is composed of two principal volumes that are differentiated from one another by their architectural language and physically separated by the common access zone which constitutes, in turn, the point of visual connection with the park.

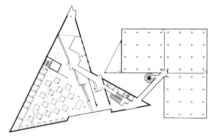

Port Vell

Paseo Joan de Borbó; Moll de la Barceloneta;
Pla del Palau; plaza Pau Vila
Jordi Henrich Monràs and Olga Tarrasó Climent, architects
Bus 14, 16, 17, 39, 45, 57, 59, 64. Metro L4 (Barceloneta)

The recuperation of the old docks as urban spaces for the use of the city has been one of the key objectives of the Ayuntamiento de Barcelona's urbanism policy over the last decade. The waterfront perimeter around the old port from the Moll d'Espanya dock to the Moll del Rellotge, on the lower edge of the Barceloneta district, has been converted into a continuous pedestrian precinct over a kilometre in length. The operation –financed by the Port Autònom de Barcelona and the Institut Municipal de Promoció Urbanística– has also involved the urbanization of the waterfront sector of the Barceloneta (paseo de Joan de Borbó), the plaza del Palau, the area around the Correos post office and the plaza Pau Vila, and the restructuring of the road network.

The vertebration of these spaces, both from the urban and the formal viewpoints, is achieved by means of the diversified utilization of the various paving materials, the small topographic movements that generate banks and slopes, the groups of trees, the lighting columns, the furniture and sculptural elements, subtly integrated into the new landscape. These artworks were created for the permanent exhibition entitled "Urban configurations" installed in the Port Vell to celebrate its inauguration: in the Moll del Rellotge, Mario Merz set up his "Fibonazzi" series; in the plaza Pau Vila, Lothar Baumgarten set the "Rosa dels Vents" compass into the pavement, with the names of the different winds in cast iron, and in the plaza del Palau, Ulrich Rückriem erected the four granite blocks of his "Untitled (Four wedges)".

Of the old buildings in the sector, the Depósito General del Comercio warehouse –now the palacio de Mar–

has been conserved and restored by the architect Eberhard Zeidler.

The rest of the quays that make up the Port Vell have been transformed by far-reaching interventions. The new Estación Marítima is currently under construction on the Moll de Barcelona, including the circular building housing the International Business Centre, designed by the architects Pei, Cobb, Freed & Partners. On the Moll d'Espanya la Rambla de Mar was created with a floating walkway (designed by H. Piñón and A. Viaplana) that connects with the paseo de Colom; a major shopping and recreation centre, the Maremagnum, was also built (to a project by Piñón, Viaplana, Jordi Mir and Rafael Coll), as well as an aquarium –the Centro del Mar–, designed by the architects Esteve Terradas and Robert Terradas, and the Cinema Imax, with a panoramic screen, designed by J. Garcés and E. Sòria.

The triangular space produced by the meeting of the Espanya and Dipòsit quays has been laid out by Pedro Barragán, monumentally overlooked by Roy Lichtenstein's sculpture "The Face of Barcelona".

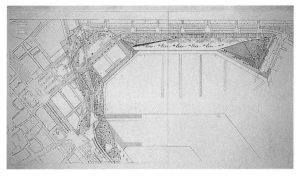

The Port Vell.

The Moll d'Espanya, with the Maremagnum building in the foreground.

The pedestrian bridge on the Moll d'Espanya.

Centre de Cultura Contemporània
Casa de Caritat　　　　　　　　　1990-1993

C/ Montalegre, 3-5

Helio Piñón Pallarés and Albert Viaplana Vea, architects

Bus 9, 14, 18, 38, 47, 58, 59, 91. Metro L1, L2, L3 (Catalunya)

The building known as the Pati de les Dones (the Women's Courtyard), part of the historic Casa de Caritad, today houses this cultural centre of international scope; the conversion involved major remodelling of the various spaces and the mutilation of the north wing of the courtyard, which was inferior in architectonic and formal quality to the other three wings. In its place, a cuboid volume contains the vertical communications core –lifts and escalators– and the entrance vestibules serving the different floors of the new building. The facade of this new construction, overlooking the courtyard, is entirely glazed, and rises up above the three original wings with an inclined inflection towards the courtyard in the manner of a cornice thus achieving remarkable visual effects and views of the old city.

The other three facades which flank the courtyard in a U-shaped layout, together with the principal exterior facade, have been restored, respectfully conserving their original morphology. The south facade of the complex is totally new, in consequence of the need to close off the building on this side after the demolition of a part of the Casa de Caritat to make way for the construction of the Museo de Arte Contemporaneo.

The injtinerary through the Centre begins in the courtyard itself, with a ramp leading down to the basement level which contains the reception area and the functions suite. The ground and first floors which, like the basement, conserve the construction characteristics of the original building, such as stone pillars and vaults, are occupied by offices, lecture rooms, shops, a bar and workshops; in contrast, the second and third floors have been thoroughly remodelled to accommodate the exhibition spaces.

144
El Corte Inglés

1990-1994

Plaza de Catalunya, 14-16; ronda de Sant Pere; c/ Fontanella
Elías Torres Tur and José Antonio Martínez Lapeña, architects
(remodelling of the existing building)
MBM and Albert Puigdomènech, architects (extension)
Bus 7, 16, 17, 22, 28, 35, 42, 47. Metro L1, L2, L3 (Catalunya)

The El Corte Inglés department store in the plaza de Catalunya has passed through a number of different phases over the years. 1962 saw the opening of the first building, situated approximately in the middle of the facade overlooking the square, and throughout the seventies this was extended in successive phases on the north side to occupy the chamfered corner of the block and part of the Ronda. The phase inaugurated in 1993 includes the new building constructed on the south corner, which has also incorporated the courtyard and a Modernista gallery –designed by Antoni Maria Gallissà– belonging to an earlier building on c/ Fontanella. The project for this new building –initially owned by a different proprietor and acquired by El Corte Inglés during the course of construction– was drawn up by MBM and Puigdomènech.

The remodelling of the building's existing facade and its extension along the Ronda de Sant Pere began in 1990 under the direction of Elías Torres and Martínez Lapeña, and there seems to have been a suggestion by the Ayuntamiento de Barcelona that there should be a degree of unity in the treatment of the two buildings, with the facades of the entire perimeter conforming a homogeneous skin.

The two chamfered corners are resolved by means of curving walls, although the language is different in each case, reflecting the creative approaches of the two teams of architects. The north corner steps back gradually towards its extremes and acts as a skin for the south corner, emphasizing the desired quality of unity. The bronze plinth and the canopy above it are continuous, and further reinforce the sense of unity. On the north corner the sign bearing the name of the department store stands out, as if chiselled into the stone, and the name appears again in silhouette on the top of the tower containing the lifts. The facade looking onto the building's interior courtyard is a handsome "curtain" of sheet metal which conceals the complex systems of services.

The interior courtyard facade.

145
"Illa Diagonal" building   1986-1993

Av. Diagonal, 555-559; c/ Numància; c/ Pau Romeva
Rafael Moneo Vallés and Manuel de Solà-Morales Rubió, architects
Bus 6, 7, 33, 34, 63, 66, 67, 68. Metro L3 (Maria Cristina)

The eastern sector of the Diagonal, from the environs of the Plaça Francesc Macià as far as the new university zone, remained relatively undeveloped until the seventies. Over the last twenty years or so, with the application to this area of a policy of implanting and encouraging the tertiary sector, planned development has taken the form of free-standing buildings, in contrast to the enclosed built fabric of the Cerdà Eixample.

This building stands on one of the latest blocks to be developed. The location of the plot, between the closed and the open blocks, and its highly unusual dimensions (with almost three hundred metres of frontage along the Diagonal), could have resulted in an overpowering architectural mass which might easily have exaggerated the break between the two typologies. In order to diminish this risk, the project

opted for a continuous line of building (in the form of a "horizontal skyscraper") which focuses on the concept of the street rather than that of the fractured or discontinuous urban space and avoids monotony by means of a carefully controlled hierarchy of volumes, the stepping in and out of the planes of the facade and an ordered modulation of the openings in relation to the regular jointing of the stone cladding on the walls. The result is one of the most impressive buildings produced by contemporary Barcelona architecture.

The "Illa Diagonal", which won the 1994 FAD Architecture award, accommodates a hotel, conference and banqueting suites, offices and shops. The building's clear commitment to engaging with its urban context is made manifest on the ground floor, traversed longitudinally by a double-height pedestrian shopping street.

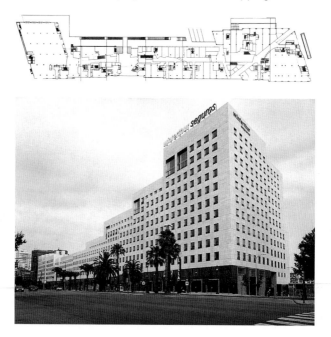

146
Apartment building

1989-1994

C/ del Carme, 55-57; c/ Roig, 28-30. El Raval
Josep Antoni Llinàs Carmona, architeco
Bus 14, 18, 38, 59. Metro L1, L3; FF.CC. Generalitat (Catalunya)

The building is situated in a sector of the historic district of El Raval that is, in both residential and the environmental terms, considerably degraded. The underlying idea of the project responds to three basic objectives: firstly, to improve the visibility and the pedestrian circulation in carrer Roig by rectifying the existing alignment of the street (in spite of the fact that local planning regulations allowed total occupation of the plot), stepping back the facades of the new building; secondly, to change the habitual built typology of the zone from the gap-site building with a continuous facade running the length of the street to one of small, virtually free-standing blocks whose disposition makes it possible to take maximum advantage of the little sunlight the plot receives; and, thirdly, to articulate the three buildings on the basis of roofed spaces with different heights and skins, on top of which are courtyards for communal use.

The layout of the apartments in plan places special emphasis on ensuring good views from the communal domestic zones such as the living and dining areas, which open onto the street by way of full-length windows and corner galleries.

Although the general treatment of the building rejects any attempt at imitating the neighbouring architecture, it does incorporate certain morphological references, such as the horizontal impost lines and the elements used to close off the window openings, in the form of folding slatted shutters, a characteristic feature of the area's 19th-century architecture.

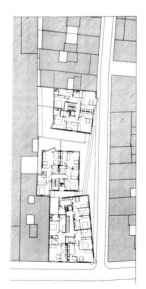

Museo de Arte Contemporáneo de Barcelona
1987-1995

Plaza dels Àngels, 1
Richard Meier & Partners, architects
Fernando Ramos Galino, collaborating architect
Bus 14, 18, 38, 59. Metro L1, L3; FF.CC. Generalitat (Catalunya)

The old Casa de la Caridad was subjected to a process of far-reaching remodelling, with the sacrifice of parts of its fabric, within the preparations for the 1992 Summer Olympic Games. Part of the building was demolished to make way for construction of the Museu d'Art Contemporani de Barcelona and the opening up of a new square.

The new building presents itself as a singular and autonomous sculptural object, standing haughtily aloof from the architectures and the urban fabric that surround it. Projecting out from the discontinuous white skin of this great cuboid form are elements which break the facades into a varied play of superimposed planes, transversely split into two volumes (with different dimensions and functional contents): a cylindrical volume (which contains the main access) and a transit space tangential to this which communicates the public square with the interior courtyard of the Casa de la Caridad.

The larger volume accommodates the circulation routes and the exhibition spaces. A corridor articulates the interior space and creates a full-height void, into which are incorporated the ramps giving access to the different floors, running parallel to the main facade, and affording visual contact between the exterior and the interior. At the southeastern corner, an opaque curvilinear volume is attached to the main construction, effectively breaking the pronounced horizontality of the complex as a whole.

In the interior courtyard of the Casa de la Caridad, during 1995 and 1996 the architects Daniel Freixes, Vicente Miranda and Vicenç Bou constructed the "Blanquerna" Faculty of Communications Sciences of the Universitat Ramon Llull (access via c/ Valldonzella, 23).

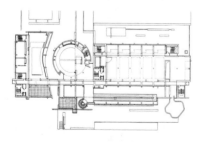

148
Terrace roof and attic
of the Casa Milà

1991-1996

Paseo de Gràcia, 92; c/ Provença, 261-265
Francisco Javier Asarta and Robert Brufau, architects
Raquel Lacuesta, art historian. Enric Mira, overall co-ordinator
Bus 22, 24. Metro L3, L5 (Diagonal)

In 1991, the Caixa de Catalunya savings bank, the present owner of this building constructed by Antoni Gaudí between 1906 and 1911, resumed the refurbishment work commenced in 1988 and undertook the restoration of the facade giving onto the courtyard in the interior of the block, the interior patios, the attic and the terrace roof. The initial studies provided essential information on the original colours and textures of the plasterwork, the mural paintings and the carpentry details, as well as the stone and ceramic trencadis claddings of the little architectural-cum-sculptural structures (stair wells, ventilation towers and chimneys) that give the roof its monumental quality.

Most of the chimneys on the terrace roof that had been added since Gaudí completed his building were removed. In the case of the attic, it was necessary to consolidate the structure and rebuild almost all of the diaphragmatic parabolic arches supporting the roof, since these had lost one or two rows of bricks when the attic space was partitioned off in 1954 to accommodate the apartments designed by J. Barba Corsini. These apartments were themselves eliminated, together with the windows that were opened in the attic to ventilate them and provide them with daylight. This made it possible to restore the attic level to its former state as a single diaphanous space, one of the most evocative ever created by Gaudí and virtually unknown to the non-specialist. Installed in this space, now opened to the public, is the Espai Gaudí –the Gaudí Space– designed by Daniel Giralt-Miracle and Fernando Marzá, which takes visitors on a journey through Gaudí's life and architecture, with an audio-visual presentation and models produced under the direction of Laura Baringo. The national cultural heritage award of the Government of Catalonia in 1997.

Forum Nord de la Tecnología　　　1993-1994

c/ Marie Curie, 135; c/ Albert Einstein. Nou Barris
Josep Benedito Rovira and Agustí Mateos Duch, architects
Bus 11, 12, 31, 32, 47, 73, 76. Metro L4 (Llucmajor)

In 1991, Barcelona City Council, by way of Barcelona Activa, S.A., organized a limited ideas competition –won by Benedito and Mateos– with the object of creating a facility with a cultural character that would be devoted to technological innovation and the promotion and diffusion of new technologies. The aims of the project were to promote the socio-economic development of this sector of the north of Barcelona and to act as the catalyst for the urbanistic ordering of the area of the old Santa Cruz mental hospital (part of which is actually occupied by the Council offices for the Nou Barris district) and the neighbouring streets.

The complex is constituted of two concrete buildings, longitudinal and parallel, linked to one another by three glazed, transparent transverse bays with sloping metal roofs. These bays are separated by two cloister-courtyards. The whole series of volumes is communicated by way of the basement and semi-basement floors, occupied by the car parks. The maximum height is virtually the same as that of the two adjacent orthogonal volumes, which formerly housed the mental hospital.

The architects Benedito and Mateos also produced the project for the fitting out of the Palau de Mar (the old Depósito General del Comercio warehouses in Barcelona's Port Vell harbour, at the start of the Passeig de Joan de Borbó) to house the Museu d'Història de Catalunya, inaugurated in 1996.

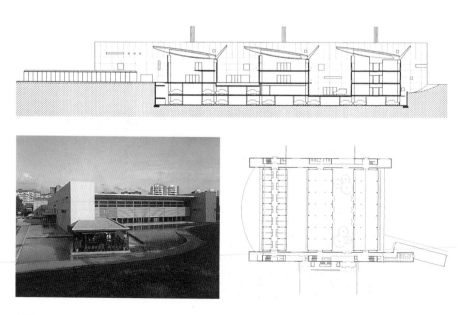

150
Biblioteca Gabriel Ferraté library   **1992-1996**

Campus Norte of the Universidad Politécnica de Cataluña
c/ Jordi Girona, 1-3
Ramon Sanabria Boix and Ramon Artigues Codó, architects
Bus 7, 54, 60, 74, 75. Metro L3 (Zona Universitària)

Situated on the southern edge of the university campus, the library stands out from the rest of the teaching buildings, in fair-faced brickwork, by the autonomy of its language and the materials which give it a representative role. The slanting geometry of the floor plans generates fragmented facades whose skin adapts to the surfaces in the form of curtain walls of glass or opaque planes, folded over in relation to the axes of the arrises. One of these folds gives rise to a very high roofed atrium (filtering the southern sun), which provides access to the street-lobby that runs the entire length of the building and divides it into two volumes: the one containing the served spaces (reading and study rooms), triangular in plan, and the other the serving spaces (services). The geometry finds its maximum expression in what asks to be regarded as the overhead facade of the building – the roof

with its sawtooth skylights, the orientation of which facilitates the entry of daylight into the reading room on the top floor.

On the west side of the library stands another of the Campus Nord constructions, the Nexus building (c/ Gran Capità, 2), a cylindrical volume with glazed surfaces designed by the architect Lluís Nadal, built in 1994.

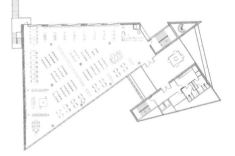

151
Banys de Sant Sebastià
1992-1997

"Club Natació Atlètic-Barceloneta"
Plaça del Mar. The Barceloneta
José Antonio Martínez Lapeña and Elías Torres Tur, architects
Bus 17, 39, 57, 59, 64. Metro L4 (Barceloneta)

The building and the Plaça del Mar occupy the plots left vacant by the demolition of the old Baños Orientales and San Sebastián baths in the Barceloneta district, whose beach underwent a major upgrading and facelift operation during the run-up to the Olympic Games in '92.

The new Banys de Sant Sebastià, a municipal development, consist of a building containing an indoor swimming pool, gymnasium, jacuzzi, saunas, solariums, restaurant, etc., and adjoining outdoor spaces (terrace with outdoor pool and games area with palm trees).

The building is conceived as a series of cuboid concrete volumes, three storeys high with sheer blind facades, interrupted only by the bands of glazing; of special note here is the great window on the first floor which allows swimmers in the indoor pool to see the sea. The intelligent use of the materials (such as the cladding of the internal walls of the indoor swimming pool with glazed perforated brick) and the beauty of some of the solutions (such as the wooden structure of the roof and the great concrete and steel gutter and gargoyle), are the

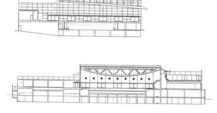

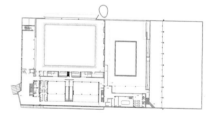

outstanding features of this minimalist building.

Following the line of the sea to the north, next to the plaza is the Sant Miquel beach, which was laid out as a seafront promenade on the basis of a project by the architects Jaume Artigues, Olga Tarrasó, Jordi Henrich and Miquel Roig, and monumentalized with a sculpture by Rebecca Horn. The intervention was awarded the FAD Prize in 1996.

San Miquel beach, Barceloneta

Parc de Canyelles

1989-1998

"Josep Ma. Serra Martí"
Via Favència. Polígon Canyelles
Cinto Hom Santolaya, architect
(with Carles Casamor, architect)
Bus 27, 31, 47. Metro L4 (Lluchmajor)

The Canyelles park is situated in the centre of the last housing estate to be built in Barcelona during the seventies, in the Guineueta Vella district, the residents of which were rehoused in the new blocks. The creation of the park is largely due to the campaign organized by the Canyelles residents' association, which managed to halt the proposal to fill the large open space with yet more housing and persuaded the City Council to devote the 4 ha to a park and amenities.

These amenities, which delimit the park, were the first to be constructed: the Canyelles market, to the west; the Urban Maintenance Centre — an elongated building designed by Enric Pericas which acts as the retaining wall for the south side of the park, which its terrace serves as a continuation of; the El Vent kindergarten (by Josep Mª Aguilera) to the north-west (all three developed by the City Council), and the church of Sant Narcís (by David Barrera) to the south-east.

The park was conceived as being at the same time a plaza-promenade. The scheme thus generated a central longitudinal axis, curvilinear in plan (carrer Antonio Machado), which creates two differentiated areas: on the steeply sloping upper part are the large open spaces the park proper and a grove of trees, as an observation platform overlooking the city; on the flatter lower part are the children's play park and the street-traders' stalls and other activities. The zones of vegetation, defined by the different types of paving, have sinuous forms which enhance the landscaping quality of the actuation and offer inter-

esting itineraries. Below the park, and forming a counter-curve in relation to the promenade, is an underground car park, whose lift and ventilation shafts project above the surface in the form of metal sculptural elements.

The original project included a lake, which has not materialized, although there is a fountain dedicated to the composer Manuel de Falla (designed by Pedro Barragán), with special effects of light, colour and sound. Close by is the sculpture *Alegries* [Joys] by the sculptor Naxo Farreras Casanovas, a monument to Maria Àngels Rivas, who was chairwoman of the residents' association during the first years of the estate's existence, and to whom the neighbourhood owes much of what it has managed to become.

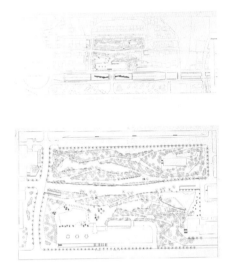

153
Jaume I building   1992-1996

Universidad Pompeu Fabra, Ciutadella Campus
c/ Ramon Trias Fargas, 23-25
Esteve Bonell Costa and Josep Maria Gil Guitart, architects
Bus 36, 41, 71. Metro L4 (Ciutadella-Vila Olímpica)

The Universitat Pompeu Fabra was created in 1990 by the Catalan parliament, and from its beginnings has opted for an urban presence; thus the first facilities were housed in refurbished buildings with an evident artistic and historical significance, a number of them located in the heart of the old city.

The Jaume I building (the name of the military barracks formerly situated in these premises) houses the departmental offices of the UPF and a library. The building occupies a typical Eixample block, with four wings configuring a large central cloister. The conversion project proposed to conserve the building, especially with respect to the original appearance of the exterior facades and those overlooking the cloister, and to adapt the interior to meet the conditions of comfort, ventilation and illumination required by the new use.

The library is in part laid out in a basement area, with access by way of a flight of stairs which leads down to a second courtyard that perforates the first, thus permitting the entry of daylight into the reading room, complemented by four cubic skylights aligned along the west side of the cloister. A second zone is constituted by the cuboid volume which rises up from the ground, letting light into the basement and generating reading rooms on the upper floors. The vertical communications cores are located at the corners of the building.

The void space between this block and the one occupied by the former Roger de Llúria barracks (similar in character to the Jaume I building) has been transformed into the UPF's Agora Rubió Balaguer, designed by the architects Jordi Garcés and Enric Sòria. In the basement, furthermore, the artist Antoni Tàpies has created the Meditation Room, his third major public work in Barcelona.

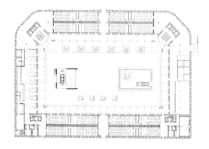

154
Auditori de Barcelona

1988-1999

Carrer de Lepant, 150; plaça de les Arts
Rafael Moneo Vallés, architect
Bus 6, 10, B21, NO. Metro L1 (Marina), L2 (Monumental)

Situated at the northern edge of the Cerdà *Eixample*, the Auditorium is one of the largest facilities in the city, together with the Hospital Clínic and the Universitat Industrial. Its simple geometry integrates it perfectly into its urban surroundings, from which it does not seek to stand out either in height or in any added decorative effect intended to monumentalize it, except for the materials themselves (a modulated combination of steel, glass and concrete), which give it a singular beauty. The main entrance, emphasized by a great projecting canopy, leads in to a spacious vestibule, an open space crowned by a translucent lantern (it might be described as a floating sculpture),

which gives access to the halls and the underground car park.

The 42,500 m² building contains a symphonic hall with capacity for an audience of 2,340, a chamber music hall, a multipurpose hall and rehearsal rooms for soloists and groups. It is also envisaged that it will house the Conservatori Superior de Música de Catalunya and the Museu de la Música de Barcelona.

The building's rectangular design contrasts with the play of geometries and the peculiar configuration of the symphonic hall, while the austerity of the exterior is compensated by the Canadian maple used for the cladding of the interior, which incorporates artificial lighting.

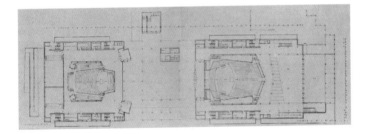

Gran Teatro del Liceo

1996-1999

La Rambla, 65

Ignasi de Solà-Morales, Lluís Dilmé, Xavier Fabré, architects

Joan Ardèvol, surveyor

Bus 14, 38, 59, 91. Metro L3 (Liceu); Guided tour, Mon-Fri (Tel: 93 485 99 00)

The first theatre, built in 1847, suffered a fire in 1861, the damaged areas being rebuilt in 1862 under the direction of the architect Josep-Oriol Mestres. The Gran Teatro del Liceo Consortium, made up of different public bodies and the Liceo's own Theatre Society, was created in 1980 with the aim of "encouraging the art of music and making it accessible to the public," as the statutes of the new association put it. Eight years later the architect Ignasi de Solà-Morales, from whom the Consortium had commissioned a preliminary plan for remodelling and extending the building (for which ten neighbouring properties had to be acquired), unveiled the model.

However, on 31 January 1994, before work could be begun, fire again ravaged the building (the main facade and various interior spaces of which were saved), a fact that hastened the work of reconstruction and amplification.

The criteria on which this operation was based had three main objectives: the installation of an advanced technology capable of providing the performance qualities needed for a contemporary opera house; the improving of the systems of access, circulation and evacuation; and the rehabilitation of the historic building so as to be compatible with a second building and its new layout, from both the formal and functional angle. Alongside the old building, the auditorium of which was almost a facsimile of the former one, a new building was erected whose facades and interior spaces are resolved in a contemporary idiom, without lapsing into historicism.

The Europa Nostra Prize and the Generalitat de Cataluña's National Cultural Heritage Prize, 2000.

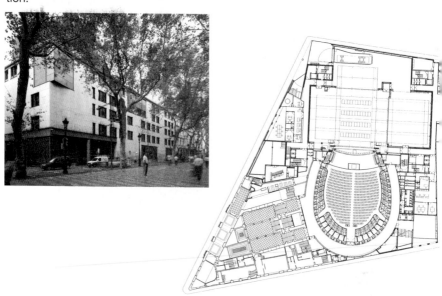

156
Barcelona Botanical Garden   **1995-1999**

Montaña de Montjuïc. Paseo Olímpico
Carlos Ferrater, José Luis Canosa, architects
Isabel Figueras, landscape architect
Bus 50, 61 E. Metro L1 (Espanya)

The Botanical Garden was constructed with European Community backing on a site of some 14 hectares used during the last hundred years as a rubbish tip. The basic aim of the project was to recycle the former tip and to convert it into a garden, with strict criteria of sustainability and the elimination of physical barriers. In order to create the new topography, recyclable and ecological materials were also used, and an integrated sprinkler system was installed whose different electro-valves are activated by a central computer. All this, plus the emergency lighting, is assisted by solar energy.

The principle of sustainability was also applied to the handling of the plants, with Mediterranean homoclimatic flowers from California, Chile, South Africa and Australia, and those from the eastern and western Mediterranean

being independently grouped together. Moreover, by basing the singular layout of the garden on botanical arbiters and on ecosystems, it was hoped to create a valuable tool in scientific, pedagogical and leisure terms. The design, which in the beginning had an artificial look to it, ended up assuming the multi-faceted dimension of nature itself, in arriving at a synthesis between the ecological balance of the plantings and an artificiality that endows the territory with a constructed infrastructure. By using a triangular grid, the landscape was gradually fragmented and certain complex demands of the project resolved, such as drainage, the pathways and watering. In this way the location itself furnishes the framework of the intervention, causing the forms of the new landscape to emerge from its own morphological and topographical features.

Worthy of note among the nexus of recent urbanised public spaces in Barcelona are the Fabra i Coats Gardens in the Sant Andreu barrio (Eva Prats and Ricardo Flores, architects, 1999); Nou Barris Central Park (Andreu Arriola and Carme Fiol, 1999-2003), and the urban development of the Paseo Central del Muelle de Barcelona (Olga Tarrasó, Jordi Henrich and Cristina Carracso, 1998-2001).

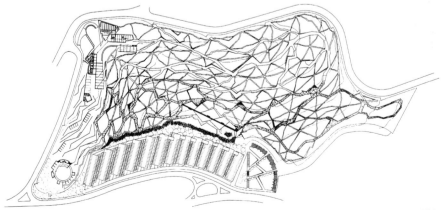

Catalonia Convention Centre · 1996-2000

Av. de la Diagonal, 661-671; c/ Torre Melina
Carlos Ferrater, José Mª Cartaña, architects
Bus 67, 68. Metro L3 (Zona Universitària)

Situated at the beginning of the A-2 motorway, this is one of the gateways to Barcelona, close to a multitude of university, sports, financial, commercial and hotel facilities, with their gardens. The axis of the Diagonal has a huge hotel capacity, and the existence at one end of it of a convention centre means making optimum use of the inducements of the city. The project aimed at endowing the complex -consisting of privately developed buildings- with a certain institutional vocation as a public amenity.

In order to adapt to the sloping topography, the building is broken down into different bodies and forms an enormous volume that, unroofed within, is double surprising for its volumetric and spatial unity, given its fragmentary outer appearance. The use of the materials, and in particular of white concrete as an almost unique exterior blanket, underlines this contrast with a cumulative composition. Two inner streets separate the three constructed bodies, allowing for visual communication between the Diagonal and the gardens of the Torre Melina, and also providing natural light to the installations. The convention centre houses, an auditorium for more than 2,000 people, the exhibition hall, identifiable from without and with a careful handling of the light, the dining rooms and complementary services (cafeteria-restaurant, offices, etc.). The diversity and functional autonomy of the installations is complemented by a series of unprogrammed spaces -access streets and plazas-, the result being a complex that functions as a social system of imbricated elements which add up to a sort of mini-city.

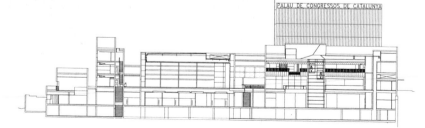

158
Theatre Institute

1996-2000

Plaza de Margarida Xirgu, (unnumbered); c/ de Lleida, 59
Ramon Sanabria, Lluís X. Comerón, architects
Bus 55. Metro L3 (Poble Sec)

The building for the new headquarters of the Theatre Institute, sponsored by Barcelona City Council, is situated within the precincts of the Flower Market and the Palace of Agriculture (public buildings built for the Barcelona International Exhibition of 1929) and forms part, along with the Municipal Theatre and the new headquarters of the Lliure Theatre, of the Theatre City. The new building is designed not to compete with the character and image established by the extant architectures, in displaying its own autonomy and modernity yet also dialoguing with its neighbours.

The programme defines two enormous functional areas, having a built surface of 20,000 m2. The first, the teaching area, is reserved for different schools and specialised activities. The second, more open in character, is reserved for the general public. Set out within the first area are the Advanced School of Dramatic Art, the Advanced School of Dance, the Conservatory of Mid-Level Dance, and such related services as the Library, Museum, Documentation Centre, parking lot, etc. The second area houses the new Ovidi Montllor Theatre and the Studio-Theatre. The building is articulated around a huge lobby-atrium in which the main entrances to each of the areas of differentiated use are situated and the various volumes enveloping this and responding to its functional diversity are defined.

A finalist in the 2001 FAD and Construmat Prizes.

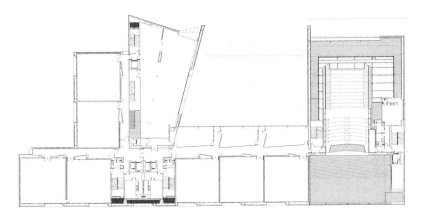

Rambla del Raval

1998-2000

El Raval, between c/ Hospital and c/ Sant Pau
Pere Cabrera Massanés, Jaume Artigues Vidal, architects
Bus 14, 38, 59, 91. Microbus 220. Metro L3 (Liceu)

The Rambla del Raval is the outcome of a planning operation included in the Revitalisation Programme of the city's historic centre promoted by Barcelona City Council. The more remote antecedents of this project are to be found in the engineer Ildefonso Cerdà's Interior Reform Plan in the 19th century, and in the other schemes which followed this during the 20th century, until 1985, when the Special Interior Reform Plan for the Raval was approved. The main objective of this intervention was to regenerate a degraded urban and social fabric by means of the cleaning up of this sector of the city and its subsequent reconstitution, together with rehabilitating the old buildings from the 18th and 19th century, which would reveal their facades for the first time.

Execution of the urbanisation project (drawn up in 1998) within the Central Plan for the Raval underwent a lengthy process involving the compulsory purchase of land, the construction of dwellings for the families affected and the demolition of certain buildings (five entire blocks defined by the Calle Hospital, Sant Geroni, Sant Pau and Cadena), following which an open area was obtained -the so-called Rambla del Raval- 317 metres long and 58 metres wide. This involves a vast urban public space delimited by restored or newly designed apartment buildings, landscaped with grass and trees, and endowed with pneumatic waste-collection systems and devices for re-utilising phreatic water for the sprinkler system. On one of the longer sides of the rambla a five-star hotel is envisaged, the design for which has been commissioned from the MBM team of architects.

160
Roger de Llúria Building

1995-2001

Universidad Pompeu Fabra. Campus de la Ciutadella

c/ Ramon Trias Fragas, 21-23

Oriol Bohigas, Josep Martorell, David Mackay (MBM), architects

Bus 36, 41, 45, 71. Metro L4 (Ciutadella – Vil·la Olímpica)

Over the last ten years the Catalan university scene has undergone enormous changes, moving from three universities to eleven, for which completely new buildings have been constructed and already existing ones remodelled. This is the case with the Roger de Llúria Building, which, like its neighbour, the Jaume I Building (cf. entry 153), was the headquarters of a former army barracks. Today it houses the Legal Sciences Faculty of the Universidad Pompeu Fabra.

The design proceeds from three basic principles: respecting the barracks' architectural identity; maintaining its external aspect (in both the facades and the roof); and creating a huge central courtyard (by first eliminating two transversal inner bodies which subdivided the existing courtyard into three sections), with two new linear buildings parallel to the longer sides of the interior of the block that accommodate classrooms and teachers' departments. The 20 x 70-meter courtyard acts as a public plaza for the students and was excavated down to the level of the underground floor (leaving the inner bays open, as if it were a ground floor) and covered by a serrated transparent roof.

City of Barcelona Prize for Architecture and Planning, 2000.

Another outstanding intervention is that undertaken on the old Convalescent Home in order to restore and upgrade the facilities of the Institute of Catalan Studies (c/ Carme, 47), planned and directed by the architect Àngel Valdés Puig between 1998 and 2000. In terms of new buildings, the extending of the Biology Faculty on the Pedralbes Campus, the work of Victor Rahola Aguadé (1999), must be cited.

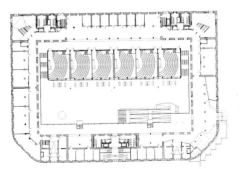

Pit-Roig Infant and Primary Education Centre
2001

c/ Aguilar, 4-14. El Guinardó

Josep A. Llinàs Carmona, architect

Bus 39

Situated in uptown Barcelona, to the northeast and very near to the Guinardó Park, the new school was built in response to a longstanding campaign aimed at the public powers by a group of parents and teachers unhappy with the temporary premises that had been hitherto used as a school. The group itself chose the site (occupied in part by another facility, a geriatric centre), and Barcelona City Council convoked an ideas competition for developing the design.

The land, on the side of Carmel Mountain, has a height difference of 12 m from the street leading to the centre to the lower edge of the plot. In this topographical factor lies the key to the scheme, which is developed as a series of terraces grounded and articu-lated in three parts, breaking up and fracturing the terrain so as to make space for a number of volumes of varying height, until each activity finds a suitable place. According to the author, the result suggests a city for children. Its integration in the surroundings, with a continuous solid wall aligned with the drive, takes note of the traditional elements delimiting the drive and some high, blank retaining walls protecting the gardens of the neighbouring dwellings.

The Gràcia Public Library (2000-2002) is by the same author. Also of note in the same El Guinardó barrio is the Mercè Rodoreda Public Library (c/ Camèlies, 76-80), designed by the architect Màrius Quintana, 1999.

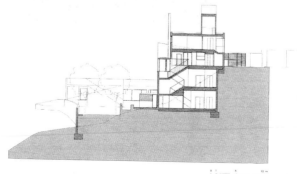

162
Sarrià Park apartment blocks   1999-2002

Ronda del General Mitre, 34-36; c/ Ricardo Villa, 11-15

Esteve Bonell, Josep Mª Gil, Francesc Rius, Josep Ribas González, Josep Ribas Folguera, architects

Bus 6, 16, 30, 34, 70, 72, 74

The requalification in planning terms of the land belonging to Real Club Deportivo Español's stadium, which was qualified as an amenity, led to a new layout and to urban change of enormous scope, with unquestionable economic and social benefits because of the building of offices and apartments and the renovation of the urban structure of the area.

On the basis of a series of previous restrictions, such as the concentration of the built volume so as to free the most public land possible, and the creation of an urban park and public amenity, a super-city block of homogeneous aspect was conceived, made up of different sized blocks and towers of between 6 and 11 floors that define tranquil interior open spaces (the park and civic plaza) connected to the outside and with a visual field which transcends and augments the precise physical dimensions of the complex. Of this complex, five buildings are intended for residential use and two for offices.

Bordering on these blocks, the so-called Fleming-Las Arcadias Block (Ronda General Mitre, 38-42) stands out, with three apartment buildings designed by the architects Jaume Bach and Gabriel Mora, and completed in 1999 (a finalist in the 2000 FAD Prizes). And in the La Ribera barrio, another apartment building giving onto the c/ del Rec and the c/ Antic de Sant Joan, 14-16, a work by the architects Antoni de Moragas Spa, Enric Jené, Enric Corbat and Mirta Weinstock (finalist in the 2001 FAD Prizes).

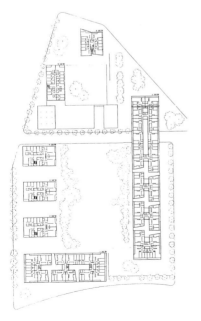

Bibliography

1999, Urbanisme de Barcelona, Ayuntamiento de Barcelona, 1999.

AB, Butlletí de la Demarcació de Barcelona, 41, 79. COAC.

AAVV, Martorell-Bohigas-Mackay: arquitectura 1953-1978, ed. Xarait, Barcelona, 1979.

AAVV, Antoni de Moragas Gallissà. Homenatge, Editorial Gustavo Gili, FAD, Barcelona, 1989.

AAVV, Barcelona, arquitectura y ciudad. 1980-1992, Editorial Gustavo Gili, Barcelona, 1990.

AC Documentos de Actividad Contemporánea, Barcelona.

Ajuntament de Barcelona, Plans i projectes per a Barcelona, 1981-1982, Barcelona, 1983.

Ajuntament de Barcelona, Barcelona espais i escultures, Barcelona, 1987.

Ajuntament de Barcelona, Urbanisme a Barcelona. Plans cap al 92, Barcelona, 1987.

Ajuntament de Barcelona, Catàleg del Patrimoni Arquitectònic Històrico-Artístic de la Ciutat de Barcelona, Barcelona (s/f) [1987].

Ajuntament de Barcelona, Memòria 1987-1991. Àmbit d'urbanisme i serveis municipals, Barcelona, 1992.

Ajuntament de Barcelona, Barcelona espai públic, 1992.

Ajuntament de Barcelona, La Barcelona del 93, 1993.

Ajuntament de Barcelona, Barcelona, posa't guapa. Memòria d'una campanya, 1993.

Ajuntament de Barcelona, 1999, Urbanisme de Barcelona, Barcelona, 1999.

Amadó, R., Domènech. L., Arquitectura para después de una guerra 1939-1949, (catálogo de exposición), COAC, 1977.

Antoni de Moragas Gallissà, homenatge. Editorial Gustavo Gili, FAD, Barcelona, 1989.

Arquebisbat de Barcelona, Labor pastoral de un gran pontificado, Barcelona, 1962.

Arquitectos, «Oriol Bohigas», 119, Consejo Superior de Colegios de Arquitectos, Madrid, 1990.

Arquitectura, 266, 278-279, 290, 297, Madrid.

Arquitectura i Urbanisme, «L'Arquitectura d'avui a Catalunya. Cases de pisos de lloguer», 3, Barcelona, enero de 1933.

Arquitectura i Urbanisme, «L'arquitectura avui a Catalunya. Cases de pisos de lloguer», Barcelona, septiembre de 1935.

Arquitecturas Bis, 6, 49, Barcelona.

Arquitectura Viva, 35, Madrid, marzo-abril 1994.

A+T, Revista de Arquitectura y Tecnología, 10, 1997.

A & V Arquitectura y Vivienda, 22, Madrid, 1990.

Barcelona. Arquitectura y ciudad. 1980-1992. Editorial Gustavo Gili, Barcelona, 1993.

Barcelona Atracción, «La arquitectura moderna en Barcelona», 242, Barcelona, 1931.

Barcelona, Metròpolis Mediterrània, 1, 23, Barcelona.

Bohigas, O: «La arquitectura moderna en España», en G. Dorfles, La arquitectura moderna, Ed. Seix y Barral, Barcelona, 1956.

Bohigas, O., Barcelona, entre el pla Cerdà i el barraquisme, Edicions 62, Barcelona, 1963.

Bohigas, O., Arquitectura española de la Segunda República, Tusquets Ed., Barcelona, 1970.

Bohigas, O., «L'arquitectura a Catalunya. 1911-1939», en E. Jardí, L'art català contemporani, Ed. Proa, Barcelona, 1972.

Bohigas, O., Reconstrucció de Barcelona, Barcelona, 1985.
Bru, E., Mateo, J.L., Arquitectura española contemporánea, Editorial Gustavo Gili, Barcelona, 1980.

Butlletí del Museu Nacional d'Art de Catalunya, 4, Barcelona, 2000.

Campus 1986-1996. Deu anys d'arquitectura universitaria a Catalunya, Generalitat de Catalunya, 1996. CAU, 7, 57, 78, Barcelona.

Capitel, A., Ortega, J., J.A. Coderch, 1945-1976, Ed. Xarait, Madrid, 1978.

Carlos Ferrater, Editorial Munilla Lería, Madrid, 2000.

CAU, «Las exposiciones del 1929, sin nostalgia», 57, Barcelona, 1979.

CAU, «Pere Benavent de Barberà, en el ocaso de la tradición», 78, Barcelona, abril de 1982.

CIC Información, «Una piscina frente al mar», 317, Barcelona, junio 1998.

Cirici Pellicer, A., L'arquitectura catalana, Ed. Teide, Barcelona, 1975.

Cuadernos de Arquitectura y Urbanismo, 1, 39, 40, 65, 68-69, 73, 78, 84, 85, 90, 91, 92, 93, 94, 103, 104, 113, 121, 131, 136, COAC, Barcelona.

Cuadernos de Arquitectura y Urbanismo, «Sert, obras y proyectos 1929-1973», 93, COAC, Barcelona, 1972.

Cuadernos de Arquitectura y Urbanismo, «GATCPAC», 90 y 94, COAC, Barcelona, 1972-1973.

Cuadernos de Arquitectura y Urbanismo, «Noucentisme: la arquitectura y la ciudad», 113, COAC, Barcelona, 1976.

DAU, 11, COAC, Lleida, verano 2000.

Díaz, Cèsar; Ravetllat, Pere-Joan, Habitatge i tipus a l'arquitectura catalana, COAC, Barcelona, 1989

Díaz, Cèsar; Ravetllat, Pere-Joan, Habitatge i context urbà, COAC, Barcelona, 1991.

Diseño de la Ciudad, 27 y 28, Barcelona, febrero-abril 2001.

Documentos de Arquitectura, «José Antonio Martínez Lapeña-Elías Torres Tur. 1976-1989». 3, COA Andalucía Oriental, Almería.

Documentos de Arquitectura, «Jaume Bach-Gabriel Mora», 5, COA Andalucía Oriental, Almería.

Documentos de Arquitectura, «Jordi Garcés-Enric Sòria», 6, COA Andalucía Oriental, Almería.

Documentos de Arquitectura, «Roser Amadó-Lluís Domènech. 1976-1989», 7, COA Andalucía Oriental, Almería, 1988.

Documentos de Arquitectura, «Josep Llinàs, 1976-1989», 11, COA Andalucía Oriental, Almería, 1990.

Domènech Girbau, L., Arquitectura española contemporánea, Ed. Blume, Barcelona, 1968.

EC Equipamientos culturales, 7 (1998) y 14 (2001), Barcelona.

El Croquis editorial, 7-8, 39, 46, 61, 64, 76, Madrid.

Fabre, J., Huertas, J. M., Barcelona, la construcció d'una ciutat, Diari de Barcelona/Plaza & Janés, Barcelona, 1989.

FAD, Premis FAD d'arquitectura i d'interiorisme 87, 88, 89, 90, 91, 92 (1988, 1989, 1990, 1991, 1992, 1993).

Fernández Alba, Antonio, La crisis de la arquitectura española. 1939-1972, Ed. Edicusa, Madrid, 1972.

Fernández Casado, Oficina de proyectos, Madrid, [1980].

Fernández-Galiano, Luis (ed.), Anuario 1993 Arquitectura Española, Madrid, 1993.

Flores, C., Arquitectura Española contemporánea. Ed. Aguilar, Bilbao, 1961

Flores, C., Amann, E., «La arquitectura de Barcelona», en Hogar y Arquitectura, 55-56, Madrid, 1964-1965.

Flores, C., Bohigas, O., «Panorama histórico de la arquitectura moderna española», en Zodiac, 15, Ed. di Comunità, Milán, diciembre de 1965.

Flores, C., Güell, X., Arquitectura en España 1929-1996. Fundación Caja de Arquitectos. Barcelona, 1996.

Fochs, C., J. A. Coderch de Sentmenat 1913-1984, Generalitat de Catalunya, Barcelona, 1988.

Garcés/Sòria, Editorial Gustavo Gili, Barcelona, 1987.

García-Martín, M., Estatuària pública de Barcelona, Catalana de Gas, Barcelona, 1984.

Garrut Romà, J.M., Itinerarios de piedad en Barcelona, Ed. Aymà, Barcelona, 1952.

Gausa, M., Cervelló, M., «Guia d'Arquitectura Contemporània. Barcelona i la seva àrea territorial, 1928-1990», en Quaderns d'Arquitectura i Urbanisme, 188-189, 1991.

Generalitat de Catalunya, *Realitzacions de la Direcció General d'Arquitectura i Habitatge i de l'Institut Català del Sòl*, Barcelona, 1988.

González Moreno-Navarro, A., «Catálogo monumental de Barcelona. Entre el búnker y la esperanza», en *ON Diseño*, Barcelona, diciembre de 1978.

González Moreno-Navarro, A., *32 monuments catalans*, Diputació de Barcelona, Barcelona, 1985.

González Moreno-Navarro, A., «El Noucentisme (1919-1959)», «La represa (1949-1979)», i «Avui», en C. Farré Sanpera (ed.), *L'Arquitectura en la Història de Catalunya*, Caixa de Catalunya, Barcelona, 1987.

González Moreno-Navarro, A., «L'Arquitectura i la gent», en *Diari de Barcelona*, Barcelona, diciembre 1989 a mayo 1990.

Grassot, Lluís de, «El azaroso paso del Rubicón de la restauración monumental en España», en *Informes de la Construcción*, n°. 427, Instituto Eduardo Torroja, Madrid, 1993.

Güell, X., Pouplana, X., Rovira, J.M., *Memòria renaixentista en l'arquitectura catalana 1920-1950*, (catálogo de exposición), COAC, Barcelona, 1983.

Hernández Cros, J. E., «Cronología de la obra realizada por los socios directivos del G.A.T.C.P.A.C.», en *Cuadernos de Arquitectura y Urbanismo*, 94, Barcelona, 1973.

Hernández Cros, J.E., Mora, G., Pouplana, X., *Arquitectura de Barcelona*, COAC, Barcelona, 1990.

Holsa, *Les noves rondes de Barcelona. Millora de la xarxa viària*, Barcelona, 1992.

Holsa, *Anella olímpica de Montjuïc*, Barcelona, 1992.

Holsa, *La Vall d'Hebron, Barcelona*, 1992.

Holsa, *La Vila Olímpica, Barcelona*, 1992.

Homenaje de Cataluña liberada a su caudillo Franco, Fomento de la Producción Nacional, Barcelona, [1939].

Hughes, R., *Barcelona*, Ed. Anagrama, Barcelona, 1992.

INDE, Informació i Debat, COAC, Barcelona, abril - mayo 2001.

Informes de la Construcción, 267, 427, 428, IET, Madrid.

Itinerarios de arquitectura 1960. Barcelona, Sitges, Santa Coloma, Barcelona, 1960.

L'Arquitectura dels anys cinquanta a Barcelona, (catálogo de exposición), Barcelona, 1987.

Lacuesta, R., «Estudios previos para la restauración de la azotea de la Casa Milà de Barcelona». *Informes de la Construcción*, 428, noviembre-diciembre 1993.

Lacuesta, R., «Studio degli elementi architettonico-Scultorei del terrazzo di Casa Milà». *Parametro, rivista internazionale di architettura*, 197, 1993.

Lacuesta, R., González, A., *Arquitectura modernista en Cataluña*, Editorial Gustavo Gili, S.A., Barcelona, 1990.

Levene, R.C., Márquez, F., Ruiz, A., *Arquitectura española contemporánea*. 1975-1990, El Croquis editorial, Madrid, 1989.

Lotus Internacional, 23, Milano, 1979.

Mackay, D., *Contradicciones en el entorno habitado*, Editorial Gustavo Gili, S.A., Barcelona, 1972.

Mackay, D., *L'arquitectura moderna a Barcelona*, Edicions 62, Barcelona, 1989.

Martinell, C., «Veinticinco años de arquitectura barcelonesa. 1908-1933», en *Barcelona Atracción*, 1933.

Martorell, Bohigas, Mackay, Puigdomènech, *La Villa Olímpica. Barcelona, 1992*, Editorial Gustavo Gili, S.A., 1992.

Miralles, F., *L'època de les avantguardes. 1917-1970*, Història de l'Art Català, VIII, Edicions 62, Barcelona, 1983.

Montaner, J. M., «La nova arquitectura de l'Eixample», en *La rehabilitació de l'Eixample*, Ajuntament de Barcelona.

Moragas i Gallissà, A. de, «La Arquitectura Catalana, hoy», en *Arquitectura 63*, ETSAB, Barcelona, 1963.

Mundo Ilustrado. Revista Hispano-Americana, 69, 73, Madrid-Barcelona, 1930-1932.

Nexus. «Gaudí-La Pedrera», 16, juliol 1996.

Nicolau Maria Rubió i Tudurí (1891-1981): El jardí, obra d'art, (catálogo de exposición), Caixa de Pensions, Barcelona, 1985.

ON Diseño, 0, 8, 33, 43, 45, 52, 65, 72, 82, 94, 102, 104, 109, 114, 116, 118, 120, 124, 125, 127, 132, 133, 135, 138, 140, 142, 143, 144, 145, 146, 153, 154, 163, 165, 173, 180, 190, 223, 224, Barcelona.

ON Diseño, "Premis FAD Arquitectura Interiorisme 2001", Barcelona, junio 2001.

OP, «Puentes II», Colegio de Ingenieros de Caminos, Canales y Puertos, Barcelona, 1991.

Pérez i Sánchez, M., (ed.), *Vint-i-cinc anys d'arquitectura barcelonina. 1914-1938*, COAC, Barcelona, 1981.

Piñón, H., *Nacionalisme i modernitat en l'arquitectura catalana contemporània*, Edicions 62. Barcelona, 1980.

Pizza, Antonio, «Jaume Mestres i Fossas, un caso de tradición inacabada», en *Composición Arquitectónica*, 7, Bilbao, octubre de 1990.

Pizza, Antonio, *España. Guía de la Arquitectura del siglo xx*. Electa, Milán, 1997.

Quaderns d'Arquitectura i Urbanisme, 144, 145, 146, 149, 150, 164, 172, 187, 188, 193, 194, 200, 210, 220, 221, 228, Barcelona.

Ràfols, J.F., *Diccionario biográfico de artistas de Cataluña desde la época romana hasta nuestros días*, Ed. Millà, Barcelona, 1951.

Ràfols, J. F., «Despliegue brunelleschiano en el novecentismo catalàn», *Cuadernos de Arquitectura*, Barcelona, II sem. 1960.

Registre d'arquitectura moderna a Catalunya 1925-1965, Col.legi d'Arquitectes de Catalunya, 1996.

Rodríguez, C., Torres J., *Grup R*, Editorial Gustavo Gili, Barcelona, 1994.

Rovira Gimeno, J. M., *La arquitectura catalana de la modernidad*, UPC, Barcelona, 1987.

Rubió, M., et al., *Nicolau M. Rubió i Tudurí (1891-1981)*, Ajuntament de Barcelona, Barcelona, 1989.

Rubió Tudurí, N. M., «L'aclimatació de l'arquitectura moderna a Barcelona», *Mirador*, 93, Barcelona, 6 de noviembre de 1930.

Rubió Tudurí, N. M., «El arquitecto Duran Reynals, artista clásico», en *Cuadernos de Arquitectura*, 65, Barcelona, 1966. (Reproducido en versión catalana en *Quaderns d'Arquitectura i Urbanisme*, 150, Barcelona, 1982).

Solà-Morales, Ignasi de; Dilmé, Lluís; Fabré, Xavier, *L'arquitectura del Liceu. Barcelona's Opera House*, Edicions UPC, Barcelona, 2000.

Solà-Morales Rubió, I., «L'arquitectura a Catalunya. 1939-1970», en E. Jardí, *L'art català contemporani*, Ed. Proa, Barcelona, 1972.

Sòria Badia, E., J. A. Coderch de Sentmenat. *Conversaciones*, Ed. Blume, Barcelona, 1979.

Suárez, Alícia; Vidal, Mercè, «L'Art Déco a Catalunya», en *Nexus*, Barcelona, desembre de 1988.

Suárez, Alícia; Vidal, Mercè, *Els arquitectes Antoni i Ramon Puig Gairalt*, Ed. Curial, Barcelona, 1993.

TA (Temas de Arquitectura y Urbanismo), «La arquitectura de Miguel Álvarez Trincado», 139, Madrid, 1971.

Tarrús, J. «Duran i Reynals: clàssic i eclèctic», en *Quaderns d'Arquitectura i Urbanisme*, 150, Barcelona, 1982.

The architects'journal, 24, junio 1996.

Ucha Donate, R., *Cincuenta años de arquitectura española (1900-1950)*, Ed. Adir, Madrid, 1980.

"Universitat, arquitectura i territori", en *INDE, Informació i Debat*, COAC, Barcelona, julio 2001.

Urrutia, Ángel, *Arquitectura española del siglo xx*. Madrid, Ediciones Cátedra, 1997.

Villoro, J., *Guia dels espais verds de Barcelona*, COAC, Barcelona, 1984.

202

Index of names

Figures in boldface type indicate the numbering of the works, while those in Roman type refer to page numbers.

Index of locations